For Citrus Only

Compiled and Edited by

Kate Armitage, Cindy Butterfield,
Jean Hurlock, Catherine Shafer

Cover photography by:
Nautilus Photography
Fort Myers, Florida

Illustrations by:
Kate Armitage

Production Staff:

Editors: Kate Armitage, Cindy Butterfield, Jean Hurlock, Catherine Shafer
Cover Photography: Nautilus Photography, Fort Myers, Florida
Illustrations: Kate Armitage
Typesetting: Stephanie Howell
Proofreading: Sylvia Murphy

The contents of this book are correct to the best of our knowledge. Advice
and recipes are made without guarantees. The authors disclaim all liability in
the use of the information in this book.

Library of Congress Catalog Number: 94-72055
ISBN: 0-9642590-0-1

Printed in the United States of America

Contents

* The Citrus Clue is used for light historical notes, culinary advise, variations of the recipes, and credits.

Acknowledgments

Kate would like to thank her children, Elizabeth and Becky, and her husband, Philip, for all their love and support, both spiritually and financially. Also to her mom and dad, Libby and Jim, who encouraged her and brought her up with a love of drawing, writing, and of course, cooking.

Cindy would like to thank Noopie, Anna, Grant, and Clint for their understanding and encouragement. She appreciates Earle and Velma Butterfield for their good taste and love of history.

Jean would like to thank her husband, Andrew, for his support and her children, Catherine, Richard, Rebecca, and Nicholas, for their patience.

Catherine would like to thank her wonderful sons, Ian and Rob, for helping harvest and test her recipes. Most of all, she would like to thank her husband, Chip, for all his love and support, and for providing encouragement when she needed it the most. Also, she would like to mention her grandfather, whose yard always brought such pleasure when his fruit trees were bearing and blooming.

We are grateful to the islanders, chefs, restaurants, and citrus growers for sharing history and recipes with us.

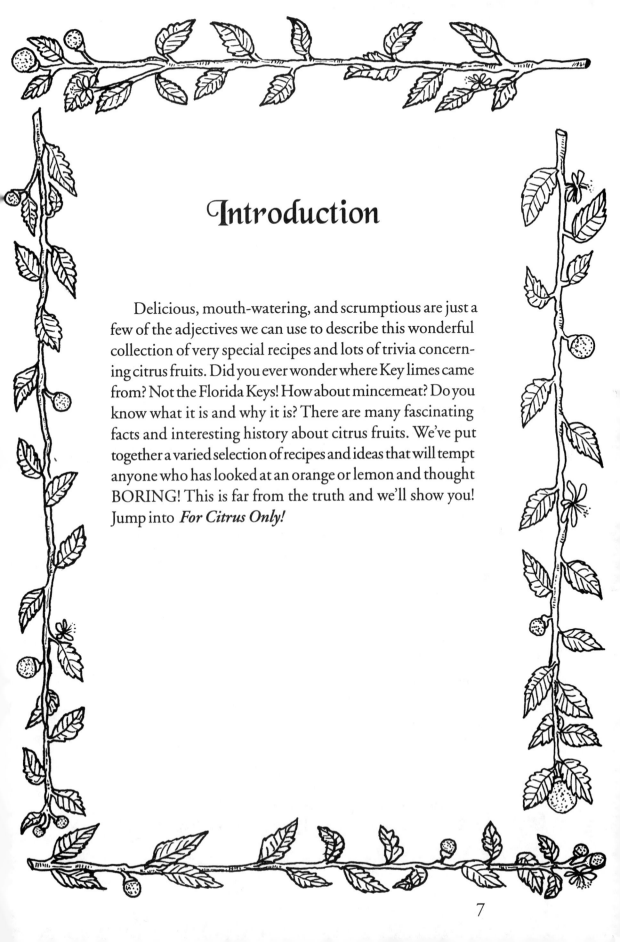

Introduction

Delicious, mouth-watering, and scrumptious are just a few of the adjectives we can use to describe this wonderful collection of very special recipes and lots of trivia concerning citrus fruits. Did you ever wonder where Key limes came from? Not the Florida Keys! How about mincemeat? Do you know what it is and why it is? There are many fascinating facts and interesting history about citrus fruits. We've put together a varied selection of recipes and ideas that will tempt anyone who has looked at an orange or lemon and thought BORING! This is far from the truth and we'll show you! Jump into *For Citrus Only!*

Citrus Fruits In History

Citrus fruits have been used in cooking and for many other uses for a long time. It is thought that the fruits originated in the Indus Valley and perhaps, concurrently in the Tigris-Euphrates Valley. From the earliest evidence of citrus fruits, we can see that fruits were an important part of diets and life. We all know now, the wonderful nutritional and vitamin value of the fruits, but early in history, oranges, lemons, and limes were grown not only for eating, but for their intrinsic beauty, scent, and religious value.

These marvelous fruits could not remain the secret of the Near and Middle East. Traders carried fruits and seeds to many different countries. Everywhere the fruits went, they were loved. The Arabs, who traveled to many parts of the Ancient World, took their cherished fruits with them, along with many exotic spices. Meats, such as mutton or goat, were fatty and bland, so many tangy recipes were concocted from the exotic juices of the citrus fruits.

The early Christians believed that the bitter taste of the lemon was poisonous, but the lemon represented the fidelity of love when seen in early Christian paintings.

It is believed that the Spaniards first brought citrus seeds to the New World in the 16th century. With Florida's conducive climate, the citrus trees flourished and, or course, are now a major industry here.

Citrus fruits took longer to catch on in Europe. Not only was the weather inhospitable to the trees, but I believe so was the cooking. Royalty and nobility who could afford the high prices, asked for the imported fruits, but the common man had to make do with the local produce. English cooking has always been a bit of a joke in the European world. It is said they can cook the best joint of meat anywhere in Europe, but their art of cooking does not extend much further. With this I disagree! Of course, being married to an Englishman, I may also be biased. The English have many, many wonderful recipes and we have included quite a few in our book.

Scurvy, long the scourge of sailors, is a nutritional disease that can easily be corrected by the addition of Vitamin C to the diet. Finally, near the end of the 18th century, the British Admiralty decreed that all sailors have lemon juice with their daily ration of rum. After 1795, lime juice was substituted, because it cost less, and hence the word "limey" was used in a derogatory sense to describe the British Seaman.

Well, when we enjoy that large glass of juice in the morning or half a grapefruit, now we can say many thanks to the traders, who, just like us, wanted a taste of home with them when they travelled abroad.

Book Source: *Food in History*, Reay Tannahill, 1973, Stein and Day Publishing.

What's In A Name?

Have you ever wonder about some of those curious names given to the many types of citrus fruits? Sandy McKenzie, co-owner of Sun Harvest Citrus, kindly provided us with a lot of very interesting information about the fruits.

The Pineapple orange was so named because of its marvelous fragrance. Packinghouse employees thought they were working amongst Hawaiian pineapples and the name stuck.

Is there any religious significance in the Parson Brown orange or the Temple orange? I don't think so, but it would be fun. Parson Nathan L. Brown was an early Florida clergyman who supplemented his clergical income with the growing and selling of oranges. The Temple orange is supposed to be a native of the Orient and sacred to the Buddhist faith. There is a story, that the seeds to the sacred trees were stolen from right under the nose of the temple guardians. WRONG! I'm afraid the origin is a lot less romantic. Mr. William Temple was an early general manager of the Florida Citrus Exchange and so the name Temple orange was born.

In 1870, an American minister in Brazil loved the flavor of the oranges so much that he sent 12 trees to Washington, DC. Usually plants are named after the locale they are found native, but the name Washington Navel has remained for over a century.

The Valencia orange is by far the most prolific of the oranges. They account for more than half the entire orange population. Valencias first arrived from England in the early 1870s. Of course, the Valencia oranges are great for making into marmalade or juice, but when they arrived in the US, there was no label on the oranges. It wasn't until an astute Spanish grower solved the mystery when he said, "That is the late orange of Valencia."

We all have heard of the famous Indian River citrus fruits, but did you know that the Indian River isn't a river, but a tidal lagoon about two miles wide and 120 miles long?

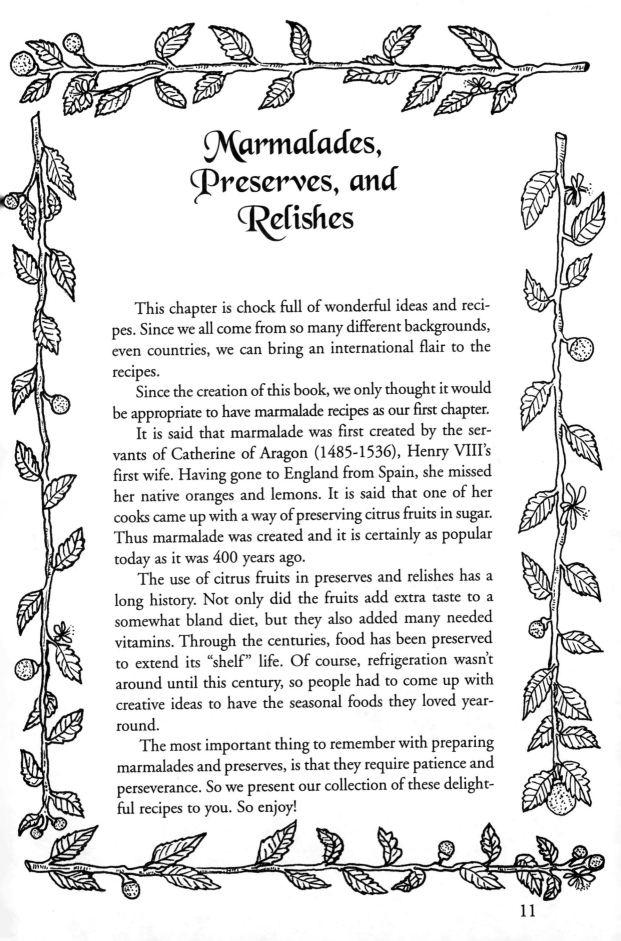

Marmalades, Preserves, and Relishes

This chapter is chock full of wonderful ideas and recipes. Since we all come from so many different backgrounds, even countries, we can bring an international flair to the recipes.

Since the creation of this book, we only thought it would be appropriate to have marmalade recipes as our first chapter.

It is said that marmalade was first created by the servants of Catherine of Aragon (1485-1536), Henry VIII's first wife. Having gone to England from Spain, she missed her native oranges and lemons. It is said that one of her cooks came up with a way of preserving citrus fruits in sugar. Thus marmalade was created and it is certainly as popular today as it was 400 years ago.

The use of citrus fruits in preserves and relishes has a long history. Not only did the fruits add extra taste to a somewhat bland diet, but they also added many needed vitamins. Through the centuries, food has been preserved to extend its "shelf" life. Of course, refrigeration wasn't around until this century, so people had to come up with creative ideas to have the seasonal foods they loved year-round.

The most important thing to remember with preparing marmalades and preserves, is that they require patience and perseverance. So we present our collection of these delightful recipes to you. So enjoy!

Four Citrus Only Marmalade

This was the marmalade that started it all. One cold January, four friends met and tried to decide what to do with tons of citrus fruit. We were overwhelmed, but not undaunted. With grim determination, we started to wash all the fruit. We seemed to be cutting it up for hours, but by the end of the day, we had the nicest marmalade jam we had tasted in years. So here is a scaled-down version of that scrumptious recipe.

6 oranges
3 pints water
1 grapefruit
2 lemons, juiced and not peeled
3 pounds sugar

Wash and dry all the fruit. Cut off the peel and put it to the side, after cutting it into shreds. Cut the fruit into sections and put in the water. Bring the water to a boil and then simmer the fruit for 1 to 1 ½ hours. After simmering, strain the water and squeeze out all the juice possible. Return to the pot with prepared shreds. Add sugar and simmer a further 45 minutes. Continue cooking the jam until when a small amount of jam can be poured on a very cold plate and you draw your finger through the jam, the mixture stays apart. Put in sterile jars and stir. Cover when cool.

Cranberry Orange Conserve

4 cups washed cranberries
(1 package)
$2/_3$ cup cold water
$2/_3$ cup boiling water
1 orange sliced with skin, seed
and cut small
$1/_4$ pound (or more) seedless
raisins
3 cups sugar ($1^1/_2$ pounds)
$1/_4$ pound walnut meats, chopped

Pick over and wash 4 cups cranberries. Add cold water; cook until skins break. Add remaining ingredients except walnuts. Bring to boiling point. Simmer 20 minutes. Add walnut meats. Makes about 4 (6 ounce) jars. If stored in the refrigerator, no need to seal with paraffin.

Citrus Clue:

Excellent with English muffins, toast, or "good off the spoon."

Orange Plum Preserve

4 pounds of cooking plums
4 oranges, grated and juiced
1¼ cups water
4 pounds sugar

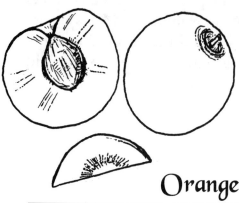

Cut the plums in half and remove the stones. Place the plum halves in a large pan and add the orange juice, rind, and the water. Bring to a boil and simmer gently for 15 minutes. Add the sugar and stir until dissolved. Boil rapidly, removing the scum until setting point is reached. Remove pan from the heat. Pour into sterile jars, cover, and label. Makes 6 pounds.

Orange Curd Tarts

½ cup butter
1½ cups sugar
2 tablespoons grated orange rind
½ cup orange juice
6 eggs, slightly beaten
1 package of tart shells

Combine butter, sugar, rind, juice, eggs, and cook in double boiler until thickened. Chill for about 30 minutes. Fill tart shells and refrigerate. Top with mint leaves and orange twist

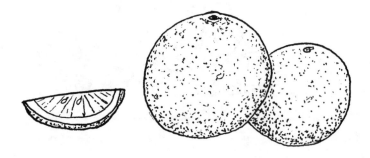

Citrus and Thyme Jelly

2 pounds oranges
2 pounds lemons
8 ³/₄ cups water
3 cups sugar
4 tablespoons fresh thyme leaves

Wash the citrus and cut into small pieces. Place the pieces of citrus in a large pan and cover with water. Boil, then reduce heat and simmer until the fruit is soft (about an hour). Strain through a jelly bag and leave to drain for two hours or better overnight. Measure the juice and pour into large pan. Add 1 cup sugar to each 2 ¹/₂ cups juice, stirring continuously bring to a boil and boil rapidly until jelly stage is reached, remove scum and stir in thyme leaves. Remove from heat and pour into warm sterile jars. Seal and label. Makes about 3 pounds.

Citrus Clue:

The jelly can be strained through a variety of cloth bags; such as cheesecloth or muslin. The Hurlock family uses sheer muslin diapers (unused, of course)!

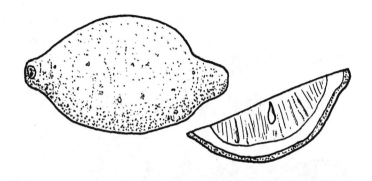

Citrus Curd

3 medium oranges
1 medium lemon (grated and juiced)
$\frac{1}{2}$ cup butter
$1\frac{1}{2}$ cups sugar
4 eggs, slightly beaten

Into a medium bowl, place grated citrus rind and citrus juice. Cut the butter into small pieces, combine with sugar and eggs and add to the juice mixture. Place a bowl over a pan of simmering water and stir until the butter and sugar are dissolved. Continue stirring until the curd will cover the back of a wooden spoon. Take care not to overcook. Pour into warmed sterile jars, cool, and store in refrigerator. Makes about $1\frac{3}{4}$ pounds.

Quick Grapefruit Curd

6 ounces grapefruit juice
$\frac{1}{2}$ cup unsalted butter
2 cups sugar
4 eggs lightly beaten and strained

Combine grapefruit juice, sugar, eggs, and butter cut into small pieces in top of double boiler. Stirring constantly until sugar dissolves and butter melts and mixture coats spoon. Pour into hot sterile jars, cool, and store in refrigerator. Makes about $1\frac{3}{4}$ pounds.

Holiday Relish

2 cups fresh orange juice
8 cups fresh cranberries
4 cups brown sugar
4 teaspoons grated orange peel
1 cup water

Boil ingredients in large pan stirring until cranberry skins burst. Remove from heat and pour into sterilized warm jars. Seal and boil in water bath for 10 minutes more. Label.

Lemon Curd

6 tablespoons butter
3 lemons
1 cup granulated sugar
3 eggs
Zest from 1 lemon

Place the butter, juice, and zest into a double boiler. Stir frequently until the sugar is dissolved and butter is melted. Whisk the eggs lightly, strain the lemon mixture into them and stir constantly in the double boiler until the mixture is creamy, about 15 minutes. Cool and place into jars like jam.

Citrus Clue:

This is very British and is great on warm fresh bread or toast.

Tomato Curd

1 pound tomatoes, chopped
1 lemon, grated and juiced
5 mint leaves
$\frac{1}{2}$ cup butter, cut in pieces
1 $\frac{1}{2}$ cups sugar
4 eggs, beaten

Place tomatoes, lemon juice, rind, and mint leaves in a saucepan and cook on low for about 10 minutes, tomatoes should be soft. Pour mixture into sieve, force mixture through into heat proof bowl. Combine with sugar, butter, and eggs. Place bowl over simmering water and stir constantly until the butter melts and the sugar has dissolved. Continue cooking until curd coats spoon. Pour into warm sterilized jars, seal, and label. Makes about 1 $\frac{3}{4}$ pounds.

Orange and Peach Chutney

2 oranges, grated and juiced
2 pounds peaches, peeled and quartered
1 $\frac{1}{4}$ cups golden raisins
1 $\frac{1}{4}$ cups onions, finely chopped
1 tablespoon ginger, grated
2 teaspoons ground cinnamon
1 teaspoon ground allspice
2 $\frac{1}{2}$ teaspoon salt
2 $\frac{1}{2}$ cups wine vinegar
1 $\frac{1}{4}$ cups sugar

Place oranges, peaches, golden raisins, onion, spices, sugar, and vinegar in a large saucepan. Bring to boil and reduce the heat and simmer for 1 $\frac{1}{2}$ hours until the chutney is thick. Remove from heat and pour into canning jars and seal. Makes 4 pounds.

Citrus Clue:

Orange trees originally came to Europe by way of the spice trail and came to Florida with the Spanish explorers. A lot of the hammocks found around the state have Seville oranges still to this day.

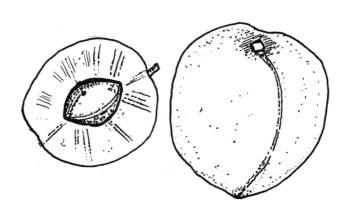

Grapefruit Chutney

4 large grapefruit, peeled and seeded (reserve peel)
2 pounds onions, thinly sliced
1 cup slivered almonds
$1\frac{1}{4}$ cups golden raisins
1 teaspoon ground ginger
1 teaspoon salt
$4\frac{1}{2}$ cups white wine vinegar
$3\frac{1}{2}$ cups sugar

Cut the grapefruit rind into thin strips and place in a large saucepan with the onions and barely cover with water. Bring to a boil then reduce the heat, simmering for 15 minutes. Pour away the water, placing the rind and onion back into the pan. Cut the prepared grapefruit and add to pan with almonds, raisins, ginger, salt, and sugar. Pour vinegar over and bring to boil, stirring until sugar dissolves. Reduce heat and simmer for about 1 hour, until the chutney thickens. Pour into canning jars and seal. Makes about 4 pounds.

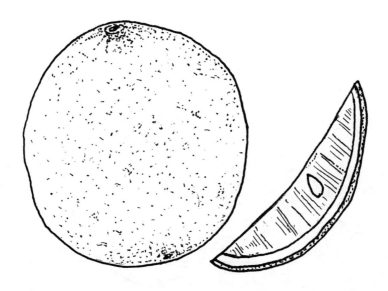

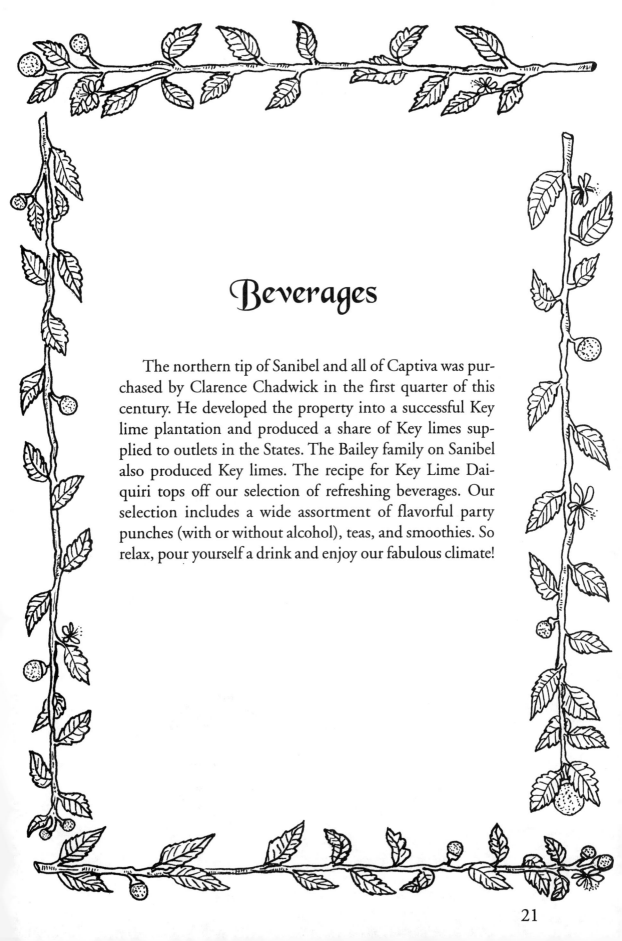

Beverages

The northern tip of Sanibel and all of Captiva was purchased by Clarence Chadwick in the first quarter of this century. He developed the property into a successful Key lime plantation and produced a share of Key limes supplied to outlets in the States. The Bailey family on Sanibel also produced Key limes. The recipe for Key Lime Daiquiri tops off our selection of refreshing beverages. Our selection includes a wide assortment of flavorful party punches (with or without alcohol), teas, and smoothies. So relax, pour yourself a drink and enjoy our fabulous climate!

C.W.'s Key Lime Daiquiri

6 ounces Key lime juice
6 ounces water
8 ounces white rum
12 ounces grapefruit juice
2 to 4 teaspoons sugar

Combine all of the ingredients and stir until sugar is dissolved. Pour mixture into freezer container and freeze overnight. When expecting guests, double the recipe and freeze for the next day.

Citrus Clue:

"C.W." recommends blending in a ripe mango, bananas, strawberries, or peaches for a tropical treat. He also suggests using 2 sugar substitutes for the sugar. "C.W." Chadwick is a colorful host at The Old History House on Captiva.

Cranberry Citrus Punch

2 quart bottles cranberry juice
1 1/2 cups lemon juice
2/3 cup sugar
One 750 ml bottle of white wine
Two 12 ounce cans of orange soda

Combine juices and sugar. Stir until sugar is dissolved. Just before serving, add wine and soda.

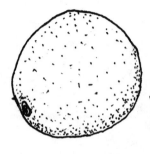 

Orange Rum

6 oranges, washed thoroughly
2 cups sugar
2 cups rum

Using orange zester remove skin from two oranges. Juice all the oranges into medium saucepan. Add zest and sugar. Bring to boil while stirring, then simmer for 5 minutes. Remove from heat and cool. Pour rum into large bottle and add orange mixture. Seal for 4 weeks. Strain and serve.

Orange Wine Zinger

2 envelopes gelatin powder
$\frac{1}{2}$ cup sugar
1 $\frac{1}{2}$ cups rosé wine
1 $\frac{1}{2}$ cups fresh orange juice
1 $\frac{1}{2}$ tablespoons fresh lemon juice
1 apple cut into $\frac{1}{4}$ " cubes
1 orange, peeled and divided into segments

Mix gelatin and sugar in saucepan with orange juice. Heat until gelatin dissolves. Remove from heat, add wine and stir. Let cool. When almost set, add orange segments and apple cubes. Pour into individual glass dishes. Serves 8-10.

Sanibel Spirits Creamsicle

3 ounces orange juice

3 ounces tropical punch of your choice

1 ½ ounces vodka

½ ounce piña colada

1 ounce creme de banana liqueur

Mix in blender and pour into chilled glass or over ice.

Citrus Clue:

Sanibel Spirits owners Pat and Roger Schmidt recommend substituting coconut flavored rum, instead of vodka, for an added twist.

Captiva Planters Punch

3 ounces orange juice
$\frac{1}{2}$ juice lemon or lime
$1\frac{1}{2}$ ounces rum
1 teaspoon powdered sugar
Dash grenadine

Mix in shaker or blender. Serve over ice. Garnish with an orange slice and a cherry.

Calamondin Liqueur

24 calamondins
2½ cups sugar
4 cups 100 proof vodka

Wash and cut the calamondins in half then remove seeds. Combine sugar and vodka. Place in large glass jar and pour mixture over fruit. Stir gently once or twice a day for 40 days. Strain and bottle.

Citrus Clue:

This liqueur is perfect to pour over ice cream or pound cake. Try this in your next margarita instead of triple sec.

Dandelion Wine

4 fresh oranges
4 fresh lemons
1 gallon dandelion blossoms
1 gallon boiling water
4 pounds granulated sugar
1 cake yeast
Bitter almond, to taste

Pour water over blossoms and let stand until blossoms rise, 24 to 48 hours. Strain into stone jar. Cut and dice oranges and lemons, put in jar along with sugar and yeast. Stir well and stand in cool place. Stir five or six times a day until fermentation ceases. Keep well covered. In two weeks, strain and add a little bitter almond. Bottle, cork very tightly, and keep in dark, cool place.

Citrus Clue:

The wine may be improved by aging in jug for six weeks.

Sunburst Smoothies

2 cups orange juice
2 frozen bananas
4 ounces strawberry yogurt

Combine juice, bananas, and yogurt in container of blender and frappe until smooth and thick.

Citrus Clue:

Try this with frozen strawberries or use fresh fruit and add ice until thick. Be creative!

Sparkling Lemon Cider

1 cup lemon juice
2 apples sliced
1 lemon sliced
2 quarts apple cider or juice
$\frac{1}{2}$ cup sugar
1 quart bottle ginger ale

Dip apple slices in lemon juice. Combine apple juice, lemon juice, and sugar. Stir until sugar dissolves. Chill. Just before serving, add slices and ginger ale. Serve over ice. Makes 3 quarts.

Citrus Clue:
An easy quick punch for festive gatherings.

Sparkling Sanibel Tropical Ice Tea

3 cups sugar
3 cups water
3 cups boiling water
$\frac{1}{4}$ cup tea leaves or 4 tea bags
3 cups orange juice
1 cup lemon juice
3 cups pineapple juice
$1\frac{1}{2}$ quarts ginger ale or club soda

Combine sugar with 3 cups water and boil for 7 minutes. Cool. Pour boiling water over tea leaves, then steep for 5 minutes. Strain and cool. Combine fruit juices, sugar syrup, and tea in punch bowl. When ready to serve, pour in ginger ale and ice. Garnish with thin slices of fresh orange and lemon. Makes 50 servings.

Citrus Clue:
Substitute fresh tangerine juice for orange juice for a brighter color.

Granny's Lovely Lemon Drink

5 cups water
1 lemon, washed
2 ½ cups sugar
1 heaped tablespoon citric acid

Pour water into a large pan. Cut the lemon in half and juice. Reserve the juice. Place the lemon halves in the water and bring to boil. Boil for 2 minutes. Add the lemon juice, citric acid, and sugar, stirring until dissolved. Cool. Mix with water to taste. Store in the refrigerator.

The Bailey Family

The Bailey family has been on Sanibel Island for 100 years, since 1894. Today, most islanders in the community have heard of or know the brothers, Francis and Samuel (Sam) Bailey. The family is an active supporter of local schools, conservation, and numerous non-profit island organizations. Sam Bailey and his brothers' experiences as boys on the island before the causeway bridge, could be a whole book by itself.

The Bailey family farmed and packed mainly Key limes and state fair prize-winning, sweet grapefruit. Sam recalls, "If you were thirsty, you would raise your hand under a hanging grapefruit. If it drops off easily into your hand, it is ripe and ready to eat. Use a jack knife to cut the top off a bit, squeeze with both hands and suck the juice."

Islanders speak about the 1926 hurricane widening Red Fish Pass and being physically damaging. "The final blow to the citrus groves was the storm of 1944. The storm had little rain, in result, the salt water was concentrated, the waves, and seaspray devastated the island. We were an island of brown. It looked as if we had a fire." explains Sam Bailey.

The "Bailey's," original store was on San Carlos Bay in a warehouse called Sanibel Packing Company. Now you can visit the original store behind the Sanibel Historical Museum. The Baileys enjoy educating people about the islands' interesting history.

Old Time Sanybel Island Key Limeade

2 cups of cool island water. Rain water collected in thick cypress-sided cisterns.

$\frac{1}{4}$ Key lime, squeezed between finger. The Key lime is solid juice compared to the pulpy Persian lime. A Key lime lover will know if you use a substitute.

1 to 3 teaspoons of island honey to taste. The honey was dark because of the palmettos. Back then, the honey was shipped out from Sanibel in barrels.

Combine all the ingredients to the best of your ability and drink. You may prefer to pour it over ice, but remember, Sam Bailey says (there was) "not a lot of ice around then!"

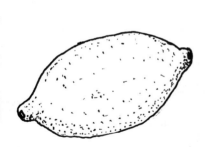

Tropic Breeze Punch

1 pint fresh orange juice
1/2 pint pineapple juice
1 lemon juiced
1 pint water
1/2 cup sugar
4 cloves
1/4 teaspoon nutmeg powder
1/4 teaspoon allspice
2 sticks of cinnamon

Slowly bring to a boil orange juice, pineapple juice, water, sugar, and spices while stirring. Let cool then add remaining juices, strain, and serve. Makes approximately 5 cups.

Russian Punch

3 cups sugar
4 quarts water
1 quart apple juice
2 quarts cranberry juice
1 1/4 cups lemon juice
1 pint orange juice
1 pint strong orange pekoe tea

Combine sugar and water and bring to a boil. Add remaining ingredients. Chill. Makes 40 servings.

Citrus Clue:

Orange pekoe tea was created by smugglers who, desperate to get tea leaves out of the orient, would hide the tea in their baskets of oranges. The fruit, by the end of the trip, imparted the orange flavor to the delicate leaves.

Lemon Pop

½ cake yeast
2 pounds granulated sugar
2 ounces
Ginger root
8 quarts boiling water
2 ounces cream of tartar
Juice of 7 lemons

Place ginger root (crushed) in pot, add sugar and boiling water, lemon juice and cream of tartar. Let stand until lukewarm, then add yeast dissolved in half cup. Stir well. Cover and let stand 8 hours in a warm room; strain through a flannel or cotton bag, and bottle. Set bottles in a cool place and chill on ice when required for use.

Citrus Clue:
In 1917, Nana made lemon pop for the first time, using this recipe.

Lemon Mint Punch

1 cup lemon juice
1 cup pineapple juice
1 cup sugar
5 drops mint extract
2 quart bottles club soda or sparkling water

Combine lemon juice, pineapple juice, and sugar; stir until sugar is dissolved. Add mint. Before serving, add sparkling water. Garnish with fruit slices for beauty.

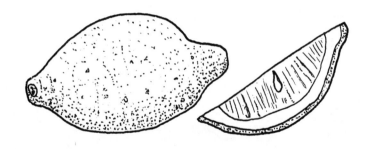

Hot Honey And Lemon Cold Remedy

1 tablespoon lemon juice
1 tablespoon honey (orange blossom is very palatable)
Boiling water
1 tablespoon rum or whiskey (optional)
Pinch of cinnamon

If you have a nasty head or chest cold, you may find that drinking this hot toddy will help your cold or at least, give you a good nights' sleep. Boil your water and in a large mug, put the lemon juice and honey. Add the hot water and liquor (if you want to) and the pinch of cinnamon. Cup the hot drink in your hands and breathe deeply, then slowly sip the drink.

Citrus Aid

With the popularity of juicing, citrus fruit naturally can be used with the juice machine. We all know that oranges, lemons, and grapefruits have many nutritional benefits, in particular, Vitamin C. When you feel a cold coming on, why don't you try juicing some of your favorite citrus fruits?

1 orange
$\frac{1}{2}$ lemon
$\frac{1}{2}$ grapefruit
$\frac{1}{2}$ pineapple

Juice together all the fruits, sip, and enjoy!

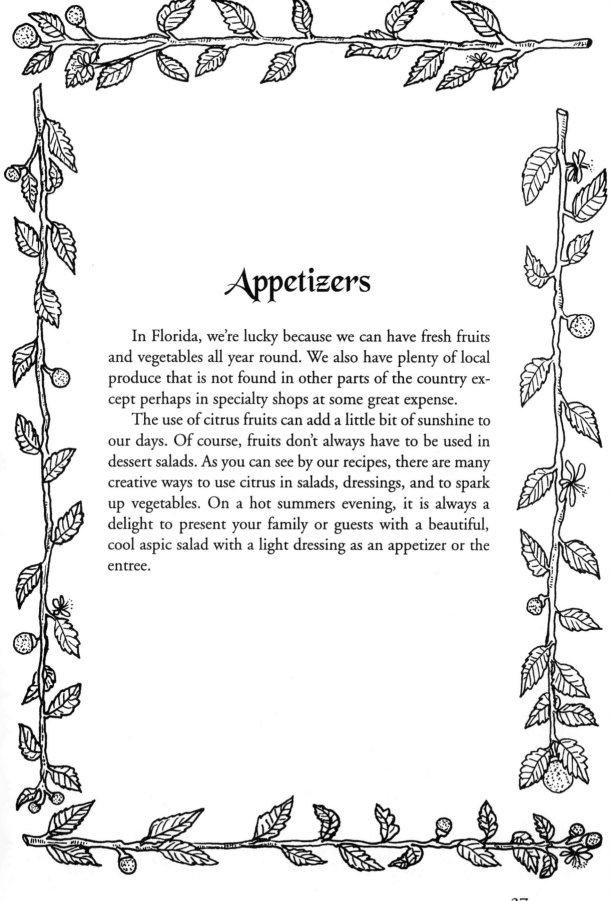

Appetizers

In Florida, we're lucky because we can have fresh fruits and vegetables all year round. We also have plenty of local produce that is not found in other parts of the country except perhaps in specialty shops at some great expense.

The use of citrus fruits can add a little bit of sunshine to our days. Of course, fruits don't always have to be used in dessert salads. As you can see by our recipes, there are many creative ways to use citrus in salads, dressings, and to spark up vegetables. On a hot summers evening, it is always a delight to present your family or guests with a beautiful, cool aspic salad with a light dressing as an appetizer or the entree.

Citrus Prawn Cocktail

12 ounces cooked peeled prawns (large shrimp)
3 tablespoons fresh lemon juice
1 cup button mushrooms, thinly sliced
2 oranges, peeled and seeded, thinly sliced
1 egg yolk
$\frac{1}{2}$ teaspoon dry mustard
Salt
$\frac{3}{4}$ cup olive oil
4 tablespoons orange juice
Grated rind of $\frac{1}{2}$ lemon
$\frac{1}{2}$ cup whipping cream, stiffly whipped
4 lemon slices for garnish

Sprinkle the prawns with half the lemon juice and marinate in the refrigerator for half an hour. Sprinkle the rest of the lemon juice over the mushrooms. Cut the orange slices in half the combine with prawns and mushrooms. Spoon into 4 decorative glasses and chill. Mix the egg yolk with the mustard and a pinch of salt. Beat in the oil, drop by drop, until thick and creamy. Stir in the orange juice and lemon rind, fold in the cream and chill. Spoon the dressing over the prawns just before serving. Garnish with the lemon slices. Serves 4.

Citrus Clue:

Try this recipe using fresh gulf 30-35 count shrimp for a gourmet treat or if you're in a hurry, purchase steamed shrimp and chill!

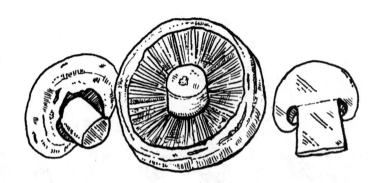

Caloosa Chutney Ball

Three 8 ounce packages cream
  cheese
1 tablespoon curry powder
1 tablespoon grated orange rind
$\frac{1}{4}$ cup orange marmalade
$\frac{1}{4}$ cup chutney

Whip cream cheese until fluffy. Stir in curry powder and orange rind. Blend with orange marmalade and shape into large ball. Cover and chill. When ready to serve, spoon chutney over ball and enjoy with crackers.

Caviar Eggs

8 hard boiled eggs
4 tablespoons butter
$\frac{1}{2}$ lemon, juiced
2 ounces caviar

Halve the eggs lengthwise, remove the yolks. Push the yolks through a fine sieve. Cream the butter with the lemon juice, the combine with egg yolks. Spoon the mixture back into the whites and place a little caviar on each egg. Decorate with parsley. Serves 4.

Citrus Meringue Soup

2 large lemons
1 large lime
2 cups water
1 orange
1 cup sweet wine
1 cup sugar
$\frac{1}{8}$ cup cornstarch
2 tablespoons cold water
2 eggs, separated

Cut and peel the citrus. Place the peel in the water and bring to a boil. Leave on simmer and cover. Simmer for 15 to 20 minutes. Discard the peel, after straining into a clean pot. Add the wine and half cup sugar. Cook this slowly until the sugar dissolves completely. Squeeze the citrus and add the juice and cornstarch to the water. Cook, stirring until it boils and thickens. Put the egg yolks in a cup. Add a few tablespoons of the hot water and mix well. Return to pot and cook until it boils. Take off the heat and pour soup into large bowl. Beat the egg whites until stiff and add the sugar to make a firm meringue. Drop by the tablespoon on top of the soup. Cover the soup so that the steam will cook the meringue. Serve hot or cold.

Citrus Clue:
This is a neat summer treat. Add extra slices of oranges or lemons to garnish.

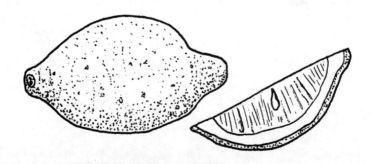

Lemon Grass Chicken Soup

1 cup sliced chicken breast
2 cups coconut milk, unsweetened
2 tablespoons nampla (fish sauce)
2 tablespoons lemon juice
1 tablespoon of sliced kha
  (oriental root)
1 teaspoon crushed chili and coriander leaves
1 tablespoon fresh chopped lemon
  grass

Combine chicken, kha, lemon grass, with coconut milk and cook until chicken is tender. Ladle into serving bowl, add nampla and lemon to taste. Sprinkle chili and coriander on top.

Citrus Clue:

Lemon grass can be substituted with a thin slice of lemon peel, grated. Kha looks like ginger root. Kha and lemon grass can be found in oriental or health food shops.

Orange Fruit Soup

3 cans (16 ounces each) pears,
drained
6 cups fresh squeezed Florida
orange juice
$1\frac{1}{2}$ teaspoons ground
cardamon
$\frac{3}{4}$ cup sour cream
5 Florida oranges, peeled and
sectioned

Puree pears in blender until smooth. (This may be done in several batches.) Pour puree into a bowl. Stir in orange juice, cardamon, and sour cream. Chill. Add orange sections. Yields 8 to 10 servings.

Citrus Clue:

Serve with assorted garnishes, such as toasted coconut, avocado slices, macadamia nuts, or orange and grapefruit sections. Submitted by Sandy McKenzie, co-owner, Sun Harvest Citrus.

Grapefruit Vinaigrette

2 grapefruit
1 cup good quality olive oil
1 tablespoon white vinegar
1 clove garlic, minced
2 egg yolks
Salt and white pepper, to taste

Using a vegetable peeler, peel only the yellow layer (zest) from one of the grapefruit. Mince a tablespoon or more of this and set aside. Squeeze the juice from both grapefruit and pour into a nonreactive sauce pan (i.e., stainless steel; not aluminum or cast iron). Bring to a boil and let bubble briskly over high heat until you have about half a cup. Let cool.

Place egg yolks in a food processor fitted with the steel blade. With motor running, drizzle in 2 tablespoons of the olive oil alternating with grapefruit juice reduction until all is used. Add garlic, grapefruit zest, and salt and white pepper to taste. You can adjust the consistency with a little juice to thin or more oil to thicken. Store in refrigerator, tightly sealed. Yields 2 cups.

Citrus Clue:

This dressing is delicious with steamed asparagus, crudites, or tossed with lettuce. It keeps in the refrigerator for a week or so. Submitted by Sandy McKenzie, co-owner, Sun Harvest Citrus.

The Moonlight Restaurant Mint and Oregano Dressing

4 large shallots, peeled

2 egg yolks

2 medium cucumbers, skinned and seeded

1 cup lightly packed oregano leaves

1 cup lightly packed mint leaves

$^2/_3$ cup rice wine vinegar

2 $^1/_2$ teaspoons salt

5 cups olive oil

In a blender, combine first 7 ingredients and blend until smooth. While the blender is still on, add olive oil in a slow steady stream. Pay special attention to adding the oil only until the dressing gets too thick to blend.

Citrus Clue:

At The Moonlight on Captiva, they serve this dressing on the house salad of bibb lettuce, toasted pine nuts, and jicama.

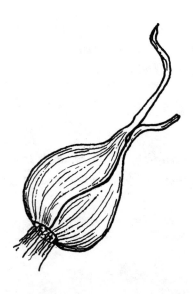

Lemon Mustard Dressing

1 lemon
Salt and freshly ground white
  pepper
$^2/_3$ cup sour cream
2 teaspoons French mustard
1 clove garlic, crushed
1 small onion, grated
1 tablespoon basil
1 tablespoon thyme

Stir the lemon juice with the salt and pepper until the salt dissolves. Combine the sour cream with the lemon juice, slowly adding the mustard, garlic, and onion. Mix in the herbs. Cool and serve.

Citrus Cilantro Dressing

$^1/_3$ cup tangelo juice
$^1/_3$ cup Key lime juice
3 tablespoons chopped fresh
  cilantro
2 tablespoons honey

Combine juices in saucepan and simmer. Add cilantro and stir in honey until well blended. Remove from the heat and let sit for 5 minutes. Chill and serve over fruit or lettuce salads. This also makes a great dip; just mix with plain yogurt or sour cream.

Pepper Strips In Lime Vinaigrette Dressing

2 red peppers
2 green peppers
¼ cup oil
1 tablespoon lime juice
1 small clove garlic
Salt and pepper to taste

Clean the peppers and cut into thin strips. In a small bowl, combine other ingredients. Toss together when ready to serve.

Citrus Clue:

This makes a very nice side dish when served with Oriental food. Libby Hayes, Kate's mom, graciously gave us this recipe.

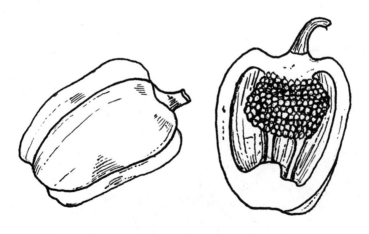

Chadwick's House Citrus Vinaigrette

6 ounces rice vinegar
2 tablespoons Dijon mustard
2 tablespoons honey
3 ounces orange juice
$\frac{1}{2}$ tablespoon pink peppercorn
1 teaspoon fresh cilantro
1 teaspoon fresh basil
1 teaspoon lemon thyme
18 ounces salad oil
$\frac{3}{4}$ teaspoon ground ginger

Place herbs, garlic, ginger, mustard, honey, and peppercorns in a cuisinart. Mix one minute (while mixing, add oil slowly). Continue to mix for 3 minutes. Store chilled. Delicious over assorted greens or pasta. Yields 1 quart.

Citrus Clue:
Chadwick's Restaurant is named after Clarence Chadwick. He previously owned the property of Captiva Island, where the restaurant is built.

Spinach Apple Salad

2 bags (10 ounces each) spinach
2 tart red apples
8 slices bacon, crisply fried and crumbled
$^2/_3$ cup salad dressing or mayonnaise
$^1/_3$ cup froze orange juice concentrate

Wash and dry the spinach leaves; tear into bite size pieces. Combine spinach, apples, and bacon. Mix salad dressing and orange juice and pour over spinach and apple mixture. Toss lightly and serve.

Citrus Clue:

Jerry's Grocery's manager suggests using mandarin oranges or fresh oranges in the place of apples.

Scallop and Orange Chili Salad

12 ounces of bay or sea scallops
4 oranges, peeled and sliced
$\frac{1}{2}$ teaspoon dried red chili flakes
3 cloves garlic, minced
$\frac{1}{2}$ teaspoon salt
10-15 mint leaves, coarsely chopped
1 fresh lime or lemon
$\frac{1}{2}$ tablespoon fish sauce

Drop scallops into pot of boiling water. Cook 2 to 3 minutes, then drain and cool. Combine the scallops and oranges slices. Add chili flakes, garlic, salt and mint leaves and thoroughly mix. Sprinkle with lime juice and fish sauce, then toss. Chill and serve.

Citrus Clue:

Our famous local Chef Noopie recommends "Nam-Pa," a well known Thai fish sauce that can be found in any Oriental market and adds a definite flavor. Try grapefruit for the oranges in this original popular recipe.

Citrus Shrimp And Calamari Salad

1 cup diced celery
$\frac{1}{2}$ cup diced yellow onion
1 cup cooked shrimp, cleaned
1 cup cooked calamari, cut small
1 tablespoon fresh lime juice
1 teaspoon heavy cream
1 $\frac{1}{2}$ cups fresh orange sections
$\frac{1}{2}$ cup mayonnaise
$\frac{1}{2}$ teaspoon mustard
$\frac{1}{4}$ teaspoon salt
$\frac{1}{4}$ teaspoon black pepper

Mix together lime juice, cream, mayonnaise, salt, and pepper. Add orange, celery, shrimp, calamari, and toss. Serves 4.

Citrus Clue:

This recipe originated from our famous local Chef Noopie. When available, use Florida Gulf shrimp.

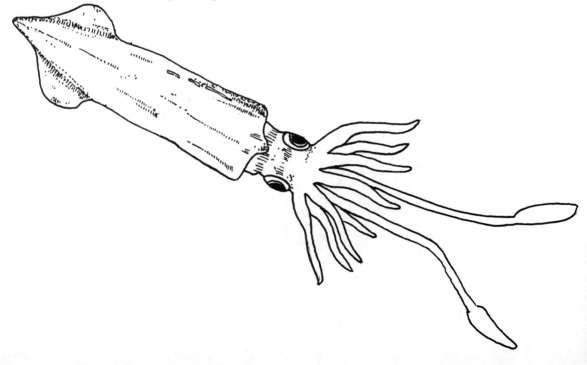

Grapefruit Endive Salad

1 large grapefruit, peeled and sectioned

1 endive lettuce, washed and thinly sliced

1 small onion, finely chopped

$\frac{1}{2}$ cup walnuts, roughly chopped

$\frac{1}{2}$ cup plain yogurt

1 teaspoon olive oil

Salt and black pepper, freshly ground

Pinch of sugar

Pinch of ground ginger

2 teaspoons orange-flavored liqueur

Place the endive in a bowl with the grapefruit and onion. Toss well and sprinkle with nuts. Whisk the yogurt with the oil adding the salt, pepper, sugar, and ginger. Stir in the orange-flavored liqueur and pour the dressing over the salad and serve. Serves 4.

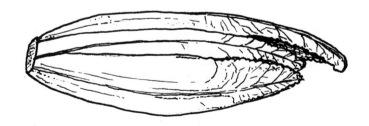

Orange Calamari Salad

2 cups cooked calamari, cleaned
  and cut into rings
2 cups fresh orange sections
2 teaspoons cilantro
1 cup diced celery
1 tablespoon fresh lemon juice
1 tablespoon sour cream
$\frac{1}{2}$ cup mayonnaise
$\frac{1}{4}$ teaspoon salt
$\frac{1}{4}$ teaspoon ginger
Fresh greens of choice

Combine orange, cilantro, and celery. Mix together lemon juice, sour cream, mayonnaise, ginger, and salt. Add cooked calamari to the first mixture, and toss. Serve on bed of fresh greens.

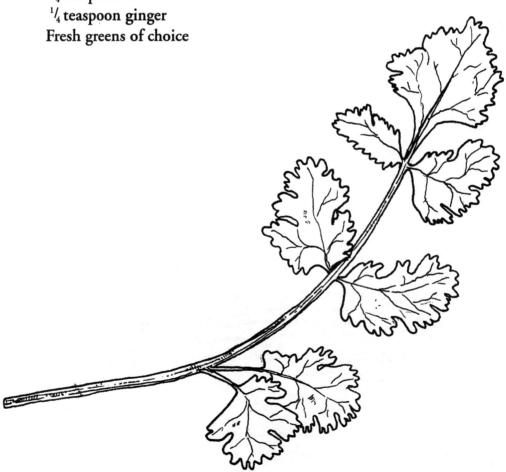

Melon, Orange, And Cucumber Salad

1 cucumber
2 oranges
½ pound seedless green
  grapes
½ cantaloupe
5 tablespoons light sour cream
1 tablespoon lemon juice
2 tablespoons sugar
Salt and pepper to taste

Wash and dry cucumber. Cut into very thin slices. Peel orange and remove all the rind. Cut into thin slices and then divide those slices into triangles. Wash and dry the grapes, save 12 for decoration. Cut the grapes in half and add to the oranges and cucumber. Cut the cantaloupe into small wedges and add. Make the dressing and pour on the salad. Toss and divide into 6 pretty serving bowls. Decorate with the remaining grapes.

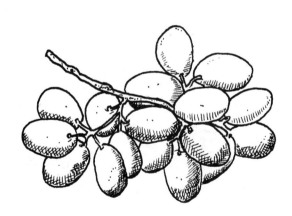

Tangerine Pecan Green Beans

⅓ cup chopped pecans
2 pounds fresh green beans
3 tablespoons sesame oil
⅓ cup chopped scallions
1 tablespoon finely chopped fresh rosemary
1 tablespoon tangerine juice
1 tablespoon grated tangerine rind

Toast pecans on a baking sheet in a 300° oven for about 5 minutes. Wash and trim beans, then steam until crisp tender. Rinse with cold water. In a wok, heat sesame oil then while stirring constantly, add scallions, green beans, pecans, rosemary, and tangerine juice. Garnish with grated rind and serve immediately.

Tropical Sweet Potatoes

1 pound sweet potatoes
$\frac{1}{2}$ cup orange juice
$\frac{1}{4}$ cup sugar
2 tablespoons all-purpose flour
4 cooking apples, sliced
$\frac{1}{4}$ cup margarine
$\frac{3}{4}$ cup orange juice

Peel sweet potatoes and cube. Combine sweet potatoes and one half cup orange juice in saucepan. Bring to a rolling boil, reduce heat to simmer, cover, and cook for about 8 minutes. Remove from heat and combine with apples. Mix together sugar and flour in small bowl. In a lightly greased casserole, lay half of the apples and potatoes, sprinkle with half of sugar and flour and dot with half of butter. Repeat with remaining ingredients and pour orange juice over all. Bake at 350° for 30 minutes.

Citrus Clue:
This dish adds a taste of sunshine to traditional Thanksgiving fare.

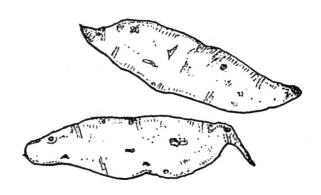

Orange Stuffed Squash

3 acorn squash
1/2 cup brown sugar
2 tablespoon butter
Juice and rind of one orange
1 teaspoon salt
Pepper to taste
1/2 teaspoon ginger

Cut the squashes in half and throw away the seeds. Put the cut sides down on a baking pan (greased) and bake at 350° for 30 minutes or until tender. When done, scoop out the pulp and keep the shells. Mix the pulp with the sugar, butter, orange juice, rind, and spices. Stuff the shells and bake, right side up, at 350° for about 15 minutes. ENJOY!

Citrus Clue:

This makes a great Thanksgiving treat and everyone will love it.

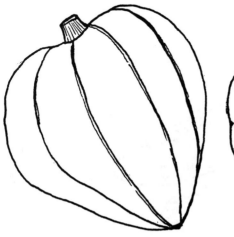 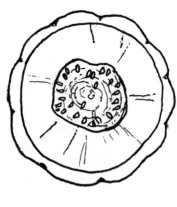

Cranberry Baskets

8-10 medium oranges
1 can jellied cranberry sauce
1 small bag frozen or fresh cranberries
Sharp paring knife

First, shave a little off the bottom of fruits to make a steady base. Then, with sharp paring knife, cut a wedge from the orange leaving at least half of the orange from the bottom of the basket and one-fourth from center top to form handle. Repeat on opposite side. Remove wedges and scoop out remaining pulp. Fill base of the basket with 2 tablespoons cranberry sauce and top with whole cranberries.

Citrus Clue:

Temple or Hamlin oranges work great for these. This makes a great family project as the older child can use the knife to cut the baskets and the younger children can scoop out the fruit and fill.

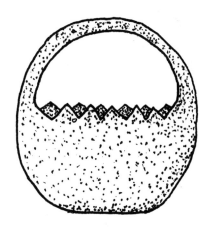

Tangy Tangelo Tea Sandwiches

1 large tangelo
One 8 ounce package cream
  cheese
$\frac{1}{2}$ cup toasted almonds
Raisin bread

Peel, section, and seed tangelo. Reserve juice. Blend 2 tablespoons juice with softened cream cheese until smooth, gently fold in sections that have been cut into bits. Spread on raisin bread and cut into small tea sandwiches.

Citrus Clue:

Tangelos are a cross between an easy-to-peel tangerine and a grapefruit. Honey Bells, Minneolas, Nova, and Orlando are a few examples.

Sauces and Marinades

Sauces and marinades are often a neglected part of our cooking routine. We know that the French love adding wonderful, but high fat sauces to many of their dishes. However, sauces do not necessarily have to be fattening and they certainly can add flavor to a somewhat ordinary piece of meat, seafood, or vegetable dish. Most sauces will store up to a week in the refrigerator and most, except those with eggs or cream, can freeze.

A good marinade should never be underestimated. A tough cut of meat or bland fillets of fish can suddenly be turned from Cinderella into the Princess. Marinades can have a delicate taste or a very spicy, tangy flavor. Marinades are very good at tenderizing. Specifically, the acid content of the citrus fruits breaks down the muscle tissues that make the meat tough. It is usually wise to marinate for 2-4 hours before cooking.

Manatee's Café Tomatillo Salsa

6 tomatillos (a type of small green tomato, the size of cherry tomatoes) finely chopped

$\frac{1}{2}$ red onion, finely chopped

1 chili, finely chopped

$\frac{1}{4}$ cup fresh cilantro

$\frac{1}{2}$ tablespoon olive oil

$\frac{1}{2}$ teaspoon fresh Key lime juice

Pinch of salt

Pinch of pepper

$\frac{1}{2}$ medium roasted red pepper or 1 tablespoon diced pimentos

Mix the above ingredients together.

Citrus Clue:

The Manatee's Café is Sanibel's newest eclectic restaurant. It specializes in "Floribean" cuisine.

Mustard Orange Sauce

¹/₂ cup mayonnaise

2 tablespoons orange juice

2 tablespoons honey

2 tablespoons creole mustard or dry mustard

¹/₂ teaspoon white vinegar

1 tablespoon fresh parsley chopped

Mix the mustard with orange juice and let stand for 15 minutes. Add mayonnaise to vinegar and honey. Blend all ingredients. Chill for one hour or more to let flavors blend. Serve on the side or on top, chill or serve at room temperature.

Citrus Clue:

Executive Chef Noopie says, "Mustard Orange Sauce tastes best with poultry or game, but you can experiment with fish."

Sage Butter And Orange Seafood Sauce

$^{1}/_{2}$ cup soft butter
4 tablespoons orange juice
1 teaspoon grated orange rind
1 teaspoon fresh sage, minced
$^{1}/_{4}$ teaspoon black pepper
$^{3}/_{4}$ cup heavy cream

In a sauce pan, heat cream with all ingredients (except butter) over a low heat. Add soft butter slowly. Serve at room temperature with any type of seafood. Yields 1 cup.

Citrus Clue:
Children may enjoy just the sauce on rice.

Pineapple And Orange Marinade

1 tablespoon orange juice
1 tablespoon grated orange rind
1 teaspoon fresh mint, finely minced
2-3 bay leaves, crushed
¾ cup rice wine vinegar
3 pineapple slices

Mix all ingredients. Heat to boiling and simmer for one minute. Let cool and use as marinade. Marinate any seafood for 30-45 minutes. Use the marinade when the fish is either baked or broiled. Can be used on poultry.

Maple And Lime Seafood Marinade

½ cup fresh lime juice
1 tablespoon maple syrup
½ teaspoon fresh ginger
½ teaspoon paprika
¼ teaspoon cracked red pepper
1 clove garlic, crushed

Mix all ingredients together and use as a marinade. Marinate any kind of seafood for 30 minutes to 1 hour. Do not broil! Yields ½ cup.

Lemon And Lime Marinade With Seafood

1 cup lemon juice
1 cup lime juice
$\frac{1}{2}$ cup minced Spanish onion
4 garlic cloves, minced
2 jalapeño peppers, minced
1 teaspoon chili powder
1 teaspoon salt
1 teaspoon sugar
8-9 fresh mint leaves, minced
$\frac{1}{2}$ teaspoon cracked black
    pepper
$\frac{1}{4}$ cup olive oil

Combine all ingredients and mix well. Add any variety of seafood, cover and allow to marinate 1 hour. Use marinade as a basting sauce when baking seafood.

Citrus Salsa

1/4 cup honey

1/4 cup fresh Florida orange juice

2 tablespoons fresh lemon juice

1 teaspoon freshly ground black pepper

2 grapefruit, peeled, sectioned, and cut into 1/2" pieces

3 green onions, finely diced

12 cherry tomatoes, quartered

In a small bowl, mix thoroughly the honey, orange juice, lemon juice, and pepper until it has a smooth, thick consistency. Set aside. In a large bowl, combine the remaining ingredients, taking care so as not to crush the pieces of fruit. Cover with the honey dressing and stir to combine. Cover with plastic wrap and refrigerate until ready to use, up to 3 days.

Citrus Clue:

This salsa is particularly suitable as a sauce served with fish which has been grilled. Also delicious on grilled chicken. Submitted by Sandy McKenzie, co-owner, Sun Harvest Citrus.

Orange Salsa: A Seafood Topping

2 cups oranges, peeled and chopped, seedless

3 tablespoons rice vinegar

$\frac{1}{2}$ cup red onion, finely minced

1 or 2 jalapeños or banana peppers; type depends on size, chopped

1 tablespoon fresh cilantro, finely chopped

1 clove fresh garlic minced

$\frac{1}{2}$ teaspoon cracked black pepper

Combine all ingredients together and let stand a few hours to develop flavor. Keep in the refrigerator. Serve cold on top or beside fish or poultry.

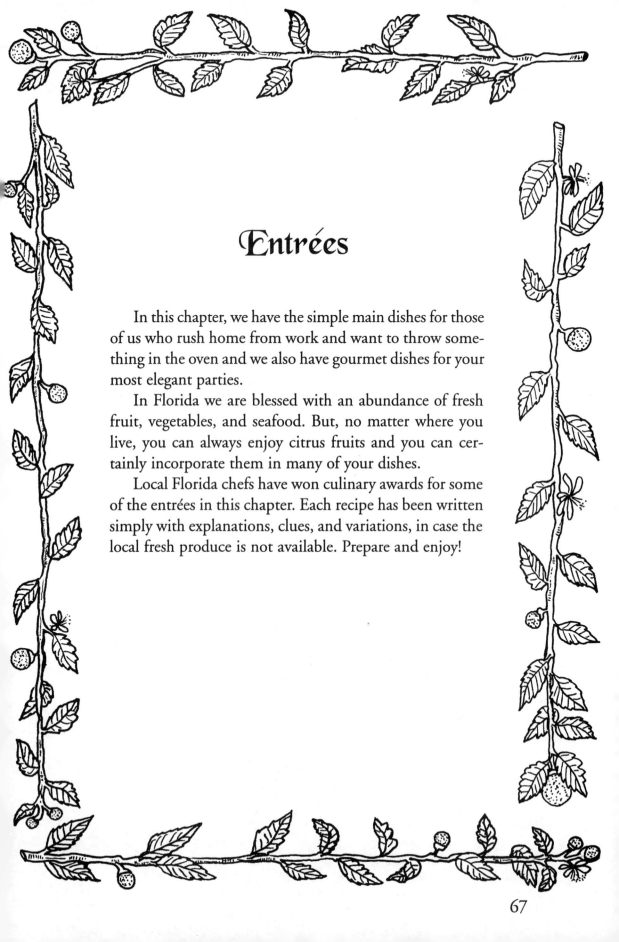

Entrées

In this chapter, we have the simple main dishes for those of us who rush home from work and want to throw something in the oven and we also have gourmet dishes for your most elegant parties.

In Florida we are blessed with an abundance of fresh fruit, vegetables, and seafood. But, no matter where you live, you can always enjoy citrus fruits and you can certainly incorporate them in many of your dishes.

Local Florida chefs have won culinary awards for some of the entrées in this chapter. Each recipe has been written simply with explanations, clues, and variations, in case the local fresh produce is not available. Prepare and enjoy!

Sautéed Grouper with Sesame Seeds and Orange

One 6-7 ounce fresh grouper fillet
3 ounces wheat flour
3 ounces cornstarch
1 large egg, beaten
1 teaspoon lemon juice
$\frac{1}{4}$ teaspoon white pepper
$\frac{3}{4}$ cup sesame seeds
$\frac{1}{4}$ cup olive oil
1 large thinly sliced orange
1 tablespoon finely minced, fresh basil

Mix the egg with lemon juice and pepper in a bowl. Put sesame seeds, wheat flour, and cornstarch in a separate bowl. Dip the fish into the egg mixture and then into the sesame flour mixture. Heat oil and when hot, quickly sauté the fish on each side. Serve fish topped with thin slices of orange and sprinkle fresh minced basil on top.

Citrus Clue:

Culinary Chef Noopie Khemkhajon prefers the use of olive oil, a monunsaturated fat, if the recipe calls for oil.

Tarwinkle's Orange Honey Glazed Snapper and Fresh Orange Beurre Blanc

Orange Honey Glazed Snapper

6-8 snapper fillets
1 cup fresh orange juice
$\frac{1}{2}$ cup honey
4 teaspoons arrowroot
White wine

Create a bloom, by mixing arrowroot with white wine until paste-like. Combine the juice and honey and simmer for 15 minutes. Add the bloom and bring to a boil. Adjust the consistency. The mixture should be like honey. Brush the mixture on the snapper fillets before broiling. Broil about 5 minutes on each side, until the fish is flaky. Serve the snapper with the Orange Beurre Blanc.

Orange Beurre Blanc

1 tablespoon shallots, minced
3 ounces white wine
4 ounces fresh orange juice
$1\frac{1}{2}$ ounces cider vinegar
1 cup heavy cream
$1\frac{1}{2}$ cups butter (softened)

Combine the shallots, wine, vinegar, and juice. Simmer until hardly any liquid is left. Add the heavy cream and reduce by $\frac{1}{3}$. Lower the heat and slowly whisk in the butter, a small amount at a time. Season with salt and pepper to taste. Creation of Chef Andrea Berry.

Baked Pompano with Key Lime-Mango Sauce

1 mango
2 squeezed Key limes
$\frac{1}{2}$ cup orange juice
$\frac{1}{2}$ cup pineapple juice
$\frac{1}{2}$ teaspoon dill
1 teaspoon teriyaki sauce
1 tablespoon honey
1 pinch of salt and white pepper
One 8 ounce pompano fillet, skin
  and bones removed
$\frac{1}{2}$ tablespoon cornstarch, add water to make paste

Combine all liquids, seasonings and bring to a low boil. Thicken by adding cornstarch paste. Add chopped mango to thickened sauce. Simmer for 3 minutes. Put pompano in greased pan. Bake at 400° for 5-8 minutes depending on the thickness of fish. Remove from oven and pour the Key lime-mango sauce over the pompano. Garnish with fresh cilantro or dill and serve proudly.

Citrus Clue:

The secret of the Key lime-mango sauce is the home-grown Key limes and mangos from Ann and Bill Walter's trees located behind their restaurant, Harbor House. The oldest restaurant on Sanibel, Harbor House Key lime pie was awarded first prize in the Chef Association's Culinary Classic.

Key West Swordfish

10 swordfish steaks

MARINADE
6 ounces red onions, diced
1 cup fresh orange juice
2 ounces Key lime juice
$\frac{1}{2}$ ounce garlic, minced
1 bunch cilantro
1 jalapeño or serrrano chili
3 ounces peanut oil
Pinch of salt
Pinch of pepper

Combine all the ingredients and mix well. Marinate the fish steaks for 2 to 4 hours. Grill the steaks about 8 minutes on each side, until the fish flakes easily.

Citrus Clue:

Chef Robert Fowler says that this marinade can be used for any firm fish steaks such as mahi-mahi, tuna, or shark. Recipe compliments of McT's Shrimp House.

Hungry Heron's Grilled Marlin Topped with Tropical Citrus Salsa

One 8 ounce Marlin steak
1 teaspoon olive oil
Salt and pepper to taste

Salsa
1 whole fresh orange, sectioned
1 whole fresh lime, sectioned
1 whole fresh lemon, sectioned
1 tablespoon red onion
1 teaspoon of fresh jalapeño,
  chopped finely, to taste
1 teaspoon fresh cilantro

Mix salsa and set aside. Rub oil on marlin. Grill 3 minutes on each side, depending on thickness. Top fish with salsa.

Citrus Clue:

The Hungry Heron's Eatery, Sanibel, is owned and operated by the DeGennaro family. Chef J.R. Underwood suggests making the salsa at least two hours ahead. The citrus acid tenderizes the mixture.

The Timber's Citrus Tuna au Poivre

Four 6 ounce tuna steaks ($^3/_4$ to 1" thick)
$^1/_2$ small lemon
1 orange
2 tablespoons oil
Coarse ground pepper
2 ounces pepper vodka (citrus vodka may be substituted for a milder taste)

Citrus Clue:

I enjoy my tuna rare to medium rare. This recipe will leave the tuna with a slight red to pink center. If you must cook your tuna past this point, be aware that it will not be as moist or tender. Try it rare! You can always cook it a little longer later on. Matt Asen, The Timber's Restaurant and Fish Market. Bon Appetit!

*If you want to impress your guests, you may flame the tuna. Be very careful and if done properly, the flames will shoot up from the pan. Remove the pan from the heat as you light with a long matchstick. The flames will go out in just a few seconds.

Using a lemon zester, cut 1" strips of orange peel being careful to take only the peel and not the white of the skin. Reserve the peels for future use. Squeeze the juice from the orange and the $^1/_2$ lemon into a shallow dish. Place the tuna steaks into the dish of juice, turning until covered with the juice. Allow them to marinate for up to an hour at room temperature or up to 3 hours in the refrigerator. Remove tuna steaks from marinade and cover with pepper. Heat the oil in a skillet large enough to hold the 4 tuna steaks. When the oil is hot, place the orange peels in the pan, stirring as they cook. They should curl up and turn brown (not black). When they are done, drain it and add the citrus marinade to the pan of orange peels. When the marinade bubbles, place the tuna steaks into the pan. Cook for about 30 seconds, then flip the steaks over and add more pepper to taste. Cook for another 30 seconds, then add the 2 ounces of pepper vodka. (At this point, you may remove the pan from the heat and set the sauce on fire as the vodka will burn.)*

Tropical Seafest Grill

1½ pounds salmon fillets
6 jumbo New Bedford scallops
12 jumbo pink gulf shrimp
(peeled and deveined)

Citrus Mango Buerre Blanc
1 ruby red grapefruit
1 Temple orange
1 lemon
3 fresh shallots, minced
1 teaspoon fresh ground pepper
1 ounce clarified butter
2 cups heavy whipping cream
1 tablespoon whole salted butter
1 pinch granulated sugar
1 mango, peeled and seeded

Cut citrus fruits in half and juice, run through a strainer to remove seeds. Puree the mango. In a medium sauté pan, heat clarified butter, adding the shallots and pepper. Sauté until caramelized and wilted. Pour in the citrus juice, with a pinch of sugar and reduce until a thick syrup is formed. Add the cream, then reduce by a third or until thick. Combine with the mango puree and reheat to simmer. Strain, then stir in the butter until melted. Grill the seafood. Place warm sauce on plate and top with seafood.

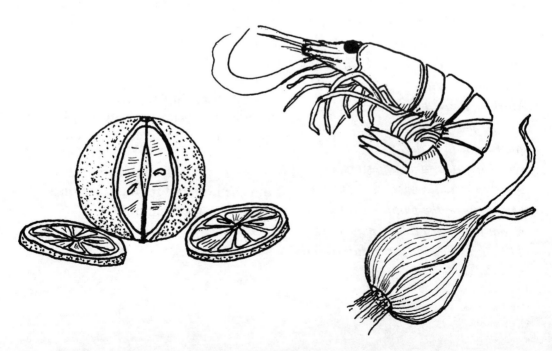

Citrus Clue:

When extracting the juice from citrus fruits, I roll the fruits on a flat surface before I cut them. This makes the juice come easier after they are cut.

When using citrus, I like to use many kinds (i.e., lemons, limes, oranges) instead of just one type. The dishes take on a more complex citrus flavor.

There are many varieties of any one citrus fruit. Try them all and create your own special recipes!

Chef Peter Abrahamson, C.W.C. was an apprentice with the 1988 U.S. Culinary Olympic team in Frankfurt, Germany. Currently, he is the executive chef at Sundial Beach Resort on Sanibel.

Oak-smoked Salmon and Baby Mixed Lettuces Tossed with Key Lime Dijon Vinaigrette

½ teaspoon Dijon mustard

½ teaspoon sugar

2 tablespoons fresh Key lime juice and zest

1 tablespoon extra virgin olive oil

2 tablespoons olive oil

3 tablespoons salad oil

⅛ teaspoon salt and pepper

⅛ teaspoon of gin and vodka

1 pound top quality, thinly sliced salmon

Lettuces (California Mesclin if available)

For vinaigrette, combine the first 8 ingredients in a blender to emulsify. Taste and adjust the seasonings to your taste, and chill. Place chilled lettuces in a large bowl. Drizzle vinaigrette over and toss to coat. Arrange a mound of lettuce in the center of four chilled plates and decoratively place salmon slices around the plate. Drizzle a dash of the vinaigrette over the salmon. Garnish with cracked pepper, Key lime wedges, and serve.

Citrus Clue:

Chef Kevin Barr, from Captiva Art Café, recommends for an added twist, adding some chopped dill, chives or your favorite herb to vinaigrette. Chef Kevin has been a chef for sixteen years and has worked and studied in Europe and the U.S.

Snapper Rolled Fillets with Lemon Wild Rice and Asparagus

2 pounds red snapper fillets

10 ounces fresh asparagus or packaged frozen, cooked and coarsely chopped

1½ cups cooked wild rice

¼ teaspoon fresh sage

¼ teaspoon paprika

¼ teaspoon black pepper

⅓ cup lemon juice

⅓ cup butter or margarine

1 cup Edam cheese, cut into small pieces

Pre-heat oven to 350°. Mix margarine with lemon juice, pepper, sage, and paprika and set aside. In a bowl, mix rice, cheese, and asparagus and add ¼ cup of the lemon margarine. Lay the fillets of fish on the cutting board flat. Divide the wild rice stuffing equally, and place portion on the wide end of each fillet and gently roll up and place seam side down in a large baking dish. Pour the rest of the butter sauce over fillets and bake for 25 minutes. Serves 4.

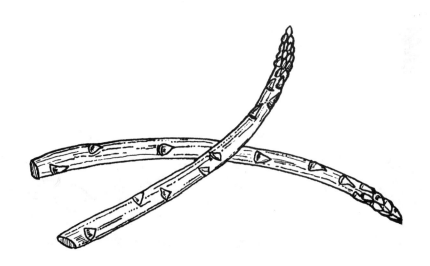

Swordfish with Orange and Lime

Four 6 ounce swordfish fillets
1 Spanish onion, thinly sliced
4 tablespoons olive oil or your favorite oil
1 bay leaf, crushed
$\frac{1}{2}$ teaspoon dried crushed red pepper
$\frac{1}{8}$ teaspoon black pepper
1 teaspoon fresh sage, finely minced
1 clove garlic, finely minced
1 tablespoon rice vinegar
$\frac{1}{2}$ cup lime juice
$\frac{1}{2}$ cup orange juice

Heat oil in heavy skillet and place a layer of the onion slices on the bottom. Place fish on onions and sprinkle with all remaining ingredients except orange slice. Cover the skillet and bring to a boil and simmer until fish flakes easily. Transfer to serving dish. Chill for at least 7-8 hours or overnight. Garnish with sliced oranges, limes, and sprinkle with fresh sage leaves.

Grouper with Orange Vinaigrette

¼ cup orange juice
4 tablespoons reduced-calorie
Italian salad dressing
4 grouper fillets
½ teaspoon orange zest
½ teaspoon butter or soy
margarine, melted

Place fillets in a baking pan. Combine orange juice and Italian dressing and pour over each fillet. Sprinkle grated orange evenly on each fillet, pour butter on each fillet. Broil or bake uncovered 8 minutes or until flaky. 350°. Serves 4.

Citrus Clue:

Orange zest is the thin outside skin of the peel. Gently shave with a vegetable peeler or use a zester and cut into pieces. New Englanders...it tastes fabulous on cod.

Key Lime Grouper

$^1/_4$ teaspoon white pepper

1 tablespoon fresh Key lime juice
   or lime

$1^1/_2$ tablespoons butter, melted

$^1/_2$ teaspoon paprika

$^1/_4$ teaspoon grated lime rind
   (lime zest)

4 grouper fillets

Sprinkle the fish with Key lime juice and white pepper. Heat the butter in a casserole serving dish. Add fillets and coat them evenly all over in the butter. Sprinkle with the paprika and lime zest and bake for 8 to 10 minutes until flakes easily. Check with a skewer. Serves 4.

Citrus Clue:

Use a zester or vegetable peeler to shave just the zest from the outside skin.

Salmon with Orange Sauce

1 pound of salmon fillets
3 tablespoons olive oil
1 clove garlic, minced
1 tablespoon lemon juice
1 whole orange, juiced
1 orange rind, finely minced
$1/_2$ teaspoon ground ginger
Salt and pepper to taste
2 teaspoons cornstarch
2 teaspoons cold water

Coat the fish fillets on both sides with 1 tablespoon of the oil and place in a baking pan, turning once until fish flakes easily, about 3-4 minutes on each side and keep warm while preparing the sauce. Heat 2 tablespoons of oil and add garlic. Over low heat, cook garlic slowly until it is soft, but not brown. Add the lemon juice, orange juice, orange rind, ginger, and salt and pepper to garlic and cook for 10 minutes. Mix the cornstarch with water and add to sauce to thicken, and pour over fish.

Gramma Dot's Carribean Mahi-Mahi

1 cup diced pineapple
2 tablespoons butter
$^3/_4$ cup diced green pepper
$^3/_4$ cup diced tomato
1 cup chicken broth
2 tablespoons corn starch
2 tablespoons soy sauce
$^1/_2$ cup vinegar
$^3/_4$ cup pineapple juice
$^1/_2$ cup sugar
1 mahi-mahi fillet

Sauté lightly pineapple, butter, green pepper, tomato, then add broth. Mix corn starch and soy together. Add vinegar, pineapple juice, and sugar. Pour liquids into sauté mixture, simmer on low heat. Grill 1 fillet until flaky. Lay fillet on serving plate. Salt, pepper, and ginger to taste. Slide sautéed fruit, vegetables, and sauce on to mahi-mahi and serve.

Citrus Clue:

Orange segments will add a new appeal! Over 40 years ago, Gramma Dot, a true grandmother, arrived by yacht and fell in love with Sanibel. Her name adorns a charming restaurant at Sanibel Marina.

Tangy Citrus Shrimp

2 pounds shrimp with shells left on
1/2 pound butter
1 cup olive oil
3 tablespoons orange juice
4 cloves garlic, minced
3 tablespoons lemon juice
1 tablespoon parsley
2 tablespoons paprika
2 tablespoons oregano
1/2 teaspoon cayenne pepper
1 tablespoon Tabasco®
3 tablespoons liquid smoke
French Bread

Lay shrimp in single layer in jelly roll pan. Melt butter in saucepan and then add the remaining ingredients and simmer gently for 4 minutes. Pour over shrimp and bake at 325° for 10 minutes. Serve with crusty french bread to dip in sauce. A messy meal, but so simple to prepare and tastes fantastic.

Citrus Clue:

Serve this meal with finger bowls and dig in! Tortuga Brand shrimp is preferable and can be obtained at a local vendor or at the home base, Beach Seafood Market, San Carlos Island, Ft. Myers Beach, Florida.

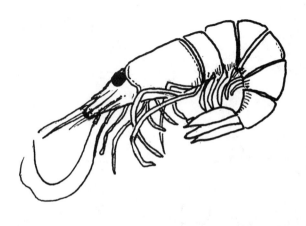

Paradise Rock Shrimp

2 pounds rock shrimp
1 cup mayonnaise
1 tablespoon Key lime juice
$\frac{1}{4}$ cup grated Parmesan cheese
1 tablespoon chopped onion
1 tablespoon chopped red bell
   pepper
Dash pepper sauce

Prepare rock shrimp by splitting the underside with shears and rinsing. Spread in pan. Blend juice, cheese, onion, red peppers, and hot sauce with mayonnaise. Spread on shrimp and broil for 5 to 8 minutes. Watch carefully to make sure shrimp don't overcook. Spread should be golden brown.

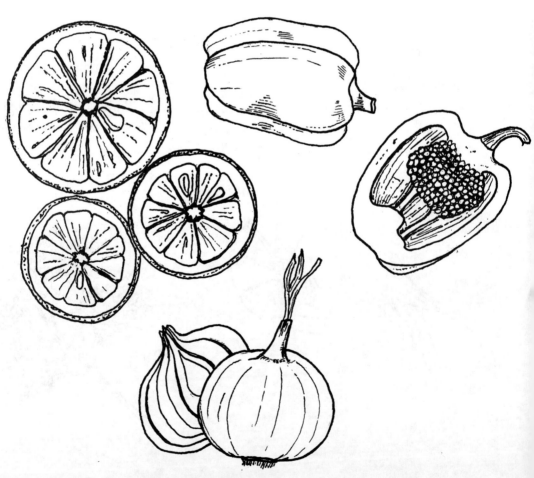

Shrimp in Citrus Cream Sauce

$1\frac{1}{2}$ pounds shrimp, peeled and deveined

1 small onion, finely chopped

3 tablespoons olive oil

3 tablespoons flour

1 cup shrimp broth

1 small lemon

1 Key lime

1 medium orange

1 cup half and half cream

1 tablespoon orange marmalade

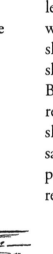

Prepare shrimp broth by boiling 1 cup water with shrimp shells and strain. Coat shrimp pieces with flour and in large skillet, sauté shrimp in $1\frac{1}{2}$ tablespoons olive oil about 2 minutes until just starting to turn white. Remove and set aside. Sauté onion in remaining oil and add juice from one half of the lemon, Key lime, and orange. Cook while stirring until sauce reduces slightly. Stir marmalade into hot shrimp broth and pour into skillet. Bring just to boil and simmer until reduced by half. Add cream and shrimp, stirring constantly until sauce thickens. Serve over rice or pasta and garnish with slices from remaining fruit. Serves 6.

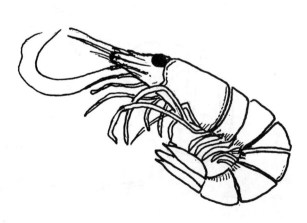

Orange Scampi Florida

$\frac{1}{2}$ cup chopped red onion
$\frac{1}{2}$ cup chopped red bell pepper
3 tablespoons orange juice
3 tablespoons sesame oil
2 tablespoons grated orange peel
1 teaspoon salt
4 scampi fillets
Fresh ground pepper

Combine the onion, orange juice, orange peel, red bell pepper, $\frac{1}{2}$ teaspoon salt in a greased baking dish. Arrange fish fillets in the mixture coating evenly. Let the fillet's marinate for an hour. Preheat the oven to 350°, turn fillets over and bake until fish flakes, 10-15 minutes depending on the thickness of the fillets. Baste occasionally. Serve with fresh ground pepper and grated orange peel.

Citrus Clue:
This is superb with scampi, but any grouper fillets will do.

Spicy Citrus Shrimp

2 ounces lemon juice
1 teaspoon grated orange rind
6 ounces picante sauce
2 ounces olive oil
$\frac{1}{2}$ teaspoon red pepper, crushed
10 drops Tabasco®
1 ounce fresh minced garlic
$\frac{1}{2}$ ounce dried parsley flakes
4 ounces orange juice
5 pounds shrimp, boiled and peeled

Combine all ingredients. Add the shrimp last. Marinate at least 24 hours. Best if chilled overnight.

Simply Sanibel Scallops

1 pound scallops
½ pound fresh mushrooms
¼ cup orange juice
¼ cup olive oil
¼ cup soy sauce
½ teaspoon ginger
½ teaspoon garlic salt

Combine orange juice, oil, soy sauce, ginger, garlic in large bowl. Marinate scallops and mushrooms for at least two hours. Broil 4 to 5 minutes in baking pan.

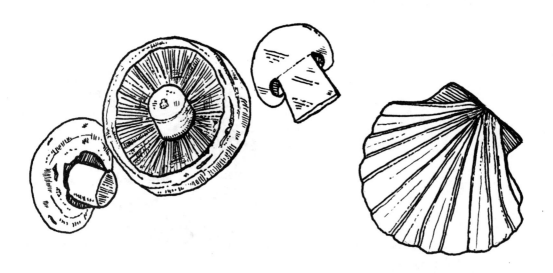

Gulfside Crab Delight

Two 8 ounce packages cream
  cheese, softened
2 tablespoons Worcestershire
  sauce
1 tablespoon lemon juice
1 small onion chopped fine
6 ounces chili sauce
1 pound fresh lump crabmeat
Dash garlic salt
Chopped fresh parsley and
  cilantro

Combine cream cheese, Worcestershire sauce, lemon juice, onion, and garlic salt. Spread on a dinner plate. Pour chili sauce over top of cheese mixture. Layer crab meat on top of chili sauce. Coat crab meat with parsley and cilantro. Cover and chill. Serve with crackers.

Citrus Clue:
This can be made the night before and is very festive for the holidays.

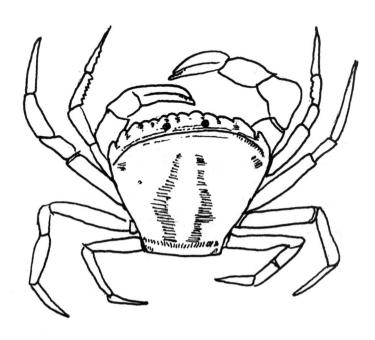

Scallops Marnier with Orange Citrus Sauce

9 ounces scallops
2 ounces blended oil
6 ounces orange juice
1 ounce Grand Marnier
2 ounces heavy cream

Sauté scallops in sauce pan with blended oil for approximately 4 minutes over medium heat. Drain excess oil and de-glaze with Grand Marnier. Add orange juice and heavy cream in same sauce pan and reduce to the consistency of a sauce. Serve scallops on large plate topped with citrus sauce and chopped parsley.

Citrus Clue:

Executive Chef, Tim Henkel, of Pippin's Bar and Grill on Sanibel suggests serving Scallops Marnier beside white rice and steamed broccoli.

Orange Cilantro Chicken

5-6 chicken breasts
1 cup orange juice
1 clove fresh garlic, minced
3 tablespoons cilantro
1 teaspoon salt
$\frac{1}{4}$ cup brown sugar
$\frac{1}{4}$ teaspoon white pepper
1 teaspoon dry mustard

Put chicken breasts in a baking pan. Mix remaining ingredients and pour over chicken breasts. Bake covered at 375° for 35-40 minutes. Uncover and baste with juice in bottom of pan. Serves 5-6.

Citrus Clue:

This is a quick and easy family favorite. Prepare in the morning and slip into the oven after work.

Tropic Citrus Chicken

1 large orange
1 large grapefruit
1 tangerine
$\frac{1}{2}$ cup shredded coconut
$\frac{2}{3}$ cup mayonnaise
1 small package herb stuffing
1 chicken, cut in pieces
One 12 ounce jar orange
  marmalade

Prepare fruit by peeling, seeding, and dividing into sections. Drain fruit and reserve juice. Blend $\frac{2}{3}$ cup of reserved juice into mayonnaise. Add coconut to the fruit sections and let marinate. Stir constantly over medium heat till it boils. Remove from heat and combine with stuffing. Spread in 13" by 9" by 2" baking pan. Top with cut up chicken. Bake in 350° oven for one hour. Melt marmalade, add fruit sections to chicken and glaze with marmalade. Broil until glaze is golden brown, watching carefully! Serves 4 generously.

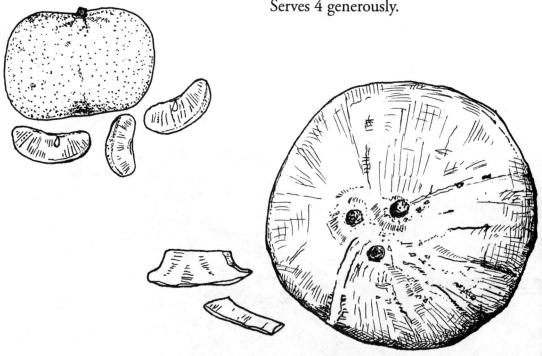

Orange Chicken

2 pounds chicken pieces (skin-less—I use chicken tenders)
1 cup orange juice
$\frac{1}{2}$ cup white wine
Italian herbs to taste
Paprika to taste
1 teaspoon of oil
1 onion, diced
1 tomato, diced
1 zucchini, thinly sliced
$\frac{1}{2}$ green pepper, diced
Salt/pepper to taste

Put the chicken pieces in a shallow baking pan and cover with juice and wine. Sprinkle with spices. Bake at 375° for 35 minutes. While the chicken is cooking, put the oil in the skillet and stir fry the onion, zucchini, and pepper. Stir constantly. When the chicken has cooked for 35 minutes, bring out of the oven and add the vegetables. Pop it back in the oven for an additional 10 minutes. When done, season to taste.

Citrus Clue:

Shop for ripe oranges first by testing for the heaviness of the fruit and sniff for a sweet smell.

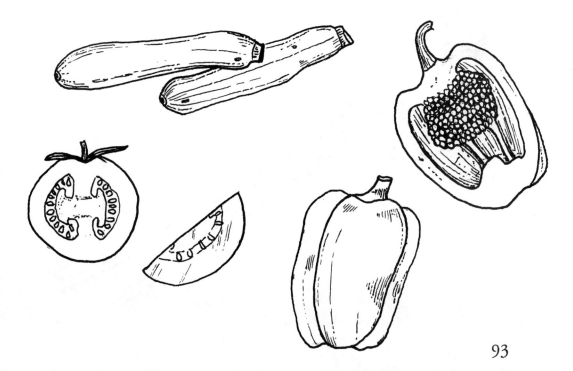

Captiva Island's Mucky Duck
Roasted Duck Ala' Orange

Two 5-6 pound ducks
Seasoned salt
4 cups aujus
1 small onion, chopped
4 pc. celery stalk, chopped
4 carrots, chopped
2 cinnamon sticks
8 cloves
$\frac{1}{2}$ cup brown sugar
$\frac{1}{3}$ cup dry sherry
1 cup frozen orange juice
  concentrate

Place ducks in deep roasting pan and coat generously with seasoned salt, bake in a pre-heated oven at 350° for approximately 2$\frac{1}{2}$ hours. Remove ducks from roasting pan, set aside and keep warm. Drain grease from roasting pan and add duck giblets, onion, celery, carrots, place on top of stove over high heat and brown. Add aujus, cinnamon sticks, cloves, brown sugar, dry sherry, and frozen orange juice. Let simmer for 30 minutes. Strain through cheese cloth into a sauce pan, bring to a boil and thicken with a corn starch roux. Cut ducks in half and remove the inside of the ducks. Place back into roasting pan and bake at 450° for 10 minutes. Remove from oven and serve with sauce and an orange slice for garnish.

Orange Beef Stir Fry

1 tablespoon olive oil
1/2 pound beef strips (1" long)
1/2 chopped onion
1 carrot (thinly sliced)
1 cup broccoli
1/2 green pepper
1 tablespoon ginger
1 teaspoon orange peel, grated
1/2 cup orange juice
1 tablespoon soy sauce
2 cups cooked rice

Heat the oil and add the beef strips. Stir fry for approximately 1 minute and remove from the pan. Add the onion, carrot, broccoli, and green pepper. Stir fry for another minute. Add the ginger and the orange peel and continue to stir fry for another minute. In a small bowl, combine the orange juice and soy sauce. Add to the vegetables and cook until the broccoli is tender. Return the beef strips to the pan and mix all together. Serve on warm boiled or steamed rice.

Citrus Clue:

Kate's mom, Libby Hayes, gave her this wonderful recipe for Orange Beef Stir Fry. Since we lived in the Orient for years, we love Oriental food.

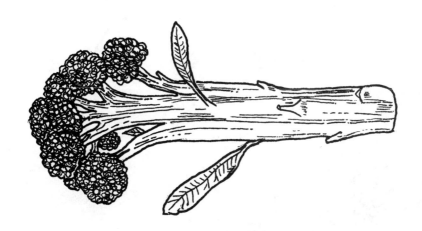

The Jacaranda's Skirt Steak Marinade

3 skirt steaks, cut into 5 ounce pieces

2 lemons and zest

$^3/_4$ cup olive oil

$^1/_2$ tablespoon garlic, finely chopped

2 tablespoons rosemary, fresh and finely chopped

2 tablespoons balsamic vinegar

1 jalapeño chili, finely chopped

$^1/_2$ tablespoon black pepper

$^1/_2$ tablespoon salt, kosher

1 tablespoon finely chopped shallots

2 tablespoons fresh sage, finely chopped

Combine all the ingredients, except the steak, in a bowl. Dip each steak in the marinade and when finished, pour the remaining marinade over the steaks and mix well. Leave the steaks in the marinade for at least 4 hours before cooking.

Citrus Clue:

Chef Robert Fowler suggests the use of kosher salt because of its lovely course texture.

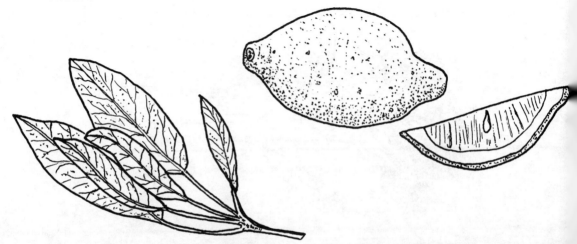

Portofino's Roast Capon with Prosciutto

6 to 7 pounds capon (organic-
free, range preferred)

$\frac{1}{2}$ lemon

Salt and pepper

$\frac{1}{8}$ teaspoon grated nutmeg

3 ounces piece of prosciutto,
coarsely chopped (cured Italian
ham, found in Italian delis)

$\frac{1}{2}$ cup dry white wine

Parmigiano® cheese

Citrus Clue:

*John Molinari, proprietor of
Portofino Restaurant, says that
both of these recipes date back as
far as the 16th century in Italy.*

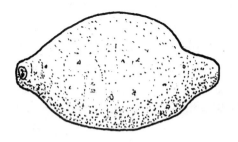

Rinse the capon under cold running water. Pat dry, trim away all
fat. Rub the inside and the outside
with lemon half. Sprinkle the cavity and skin of capon with salt, pepper, and nutmeg. Put the prosciutto
into the cavity. Place capon on the
platter, cover with plastic wrap.
Refrigerate overnight. Preheat the
oven to 325° and put the capon
breast down in a shallow roasting
pan. Roast for $2\frac{1}{2}$ to 3 hours. (Meat
thermometer will read 170°) After
the first 30 minutes, begin basting
capon with white wine every 20
minutes until you've used up all the
wine. Then start basting with
marsala and the pan juices. 30 minutes before the capon is done, turn
over to brown the breast. When
done, let the capon rest for 10 to
15 minutes. Take prosciutto out of
the cavity and set aside. Carve the
capon by slicing the breast into
thick slices and dividing the leg
meat into 3 or 4 pieces. Place capon on platter and cover with
juices. Sprinkle capon with prosciutto. Serve alone or with
tagliatelle (see next recipe).

Portofino's Tagliatelle Con Arance
(Tagliatelle with carmelized oranges)

1 quart water

2 large oranges

8 tablespoons unsalted butter

1½ cups orange juice

⅔ cup sugar

⅛ teaspoon fresh ground pepper

6 quarts salted water

1 pound imported dried tagliatelle pasta

3 tablespoons sugar

1 teaspoon ground cinnamon

⅔ cup fresh grated Parmigiano® cheese

1 cup whole blanched almonds, toasted and chopped

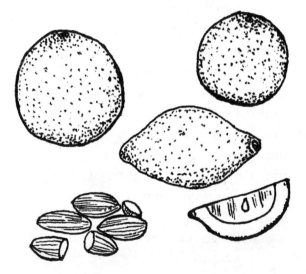

Bring one quart of water to a boil. Remove the zest from the oranges in long, thin strips, and add to the boiling water for an additional 3 minutes. Remove the zest, cool and set aside. Melt the butter in a large skillet over a medium heat. Stir in ¼ cup of orange juice and ⅔ cup sugar. Melt the sugar with the orange juice mixture. Stir in teaspoons of orange juice frequently, to keep the orange juice from crystallizing (save ⅓ cup of juice for finishing the sauce). Once the sugar has dissolved, turn up the heat and cook until it reaches a golden amber color. Blend in the pepper and ½ the zest and cook for a few seconds. At arms length, add the rest of the juice, mix and take off the heat. Next, bring the water to a boil and cook the pasta till al dente. Drain. Reheat the orange mixture till bubbly and add pasta. Toss well. Serve on a warmed platter and sprinkle with sugar, cinnamon, cheese, almonds, and zest.

(Continued on next page)

Portofino's Tagliatelle Con Arance
(Continued)

This pasta dish can be either a wonderful side dish or an unexpected dessert. If serving with the capon, place on top of pasta and serve. As a dessert, serve in warmed dessert bowls, piping hot.

Citrus Clue:

The sauce can be made several hours ahead of time and reheated. You can substitute fettucine for tagliatelle. Tagliatelle can easily be found in Italian delis.

Sunset Grilled Veal Chop Stuffed with Smoked Mozzarella Citrus Salsa

Four 12 ounce veal chops
$\frac{1}{2}$ juice of one lime
2 tangerines, sectioned
1 grapefruit, sectioned and seeded
3 kumquats, diced
1 jalapeño, seeded and diced
4-5 sprigs chopped fresh mint
$\frac{1}{4}$ cup citron vodka
1 cup smoked mozzarella, shredded
Bamboo skewers
Dashes of olive oil, salt, and pepper

Take lime, tangerines, grapefruit, kumquats, jalapeño, mint, citron vodka, and cheese and mix together the day before to marinate. Prepare veal chops by making a $2\frac{1}{2}$" to 3" slit in center of the meat to bone. Using a large spoon, stuff pocket with salsa, then take skewer and thread through the outer rim of the cut to close pocket. Rub chops with olive oil, lightly salt and pepper. Grill stuffed chops on medium high heat for 7-8 minutes per side. Be careful to turn cut side up when flipping over.

Citrus Clue:

Citron vodka is a light citrus flavored vodka. Sunset Grill on Blind Pass, is owned by Larry Thompson and Bruce Baker with Chef John Feagens serving as manager. A citron is a huge, round, very sour, lumpy lemon.

Citrus Tabbouleh

2 cups bulgur
1 cup tangelo juice
1 bunch parsley
1 medium tomato
1 bunch mint
1 bunch scallions
$\frac{1}{4}$ cup tangelo juice
2 tablespoons olive oil

Bring tangelo juice to a boil, stir gently into bulgur and let soak for about 30 minutes until juice is absorbed. While bulgur is soaking, chop and toss together parsley, tomato, mint, and scallions. Add juice and olive oil and let flavors blend. Combine with prepared bulgur and chill for at least 30 minutes.

Citrus Clue:

Bulgur is wheat that has been parboiled, cracked, and dried.

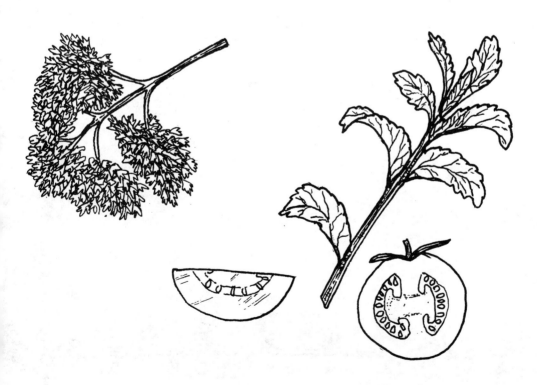

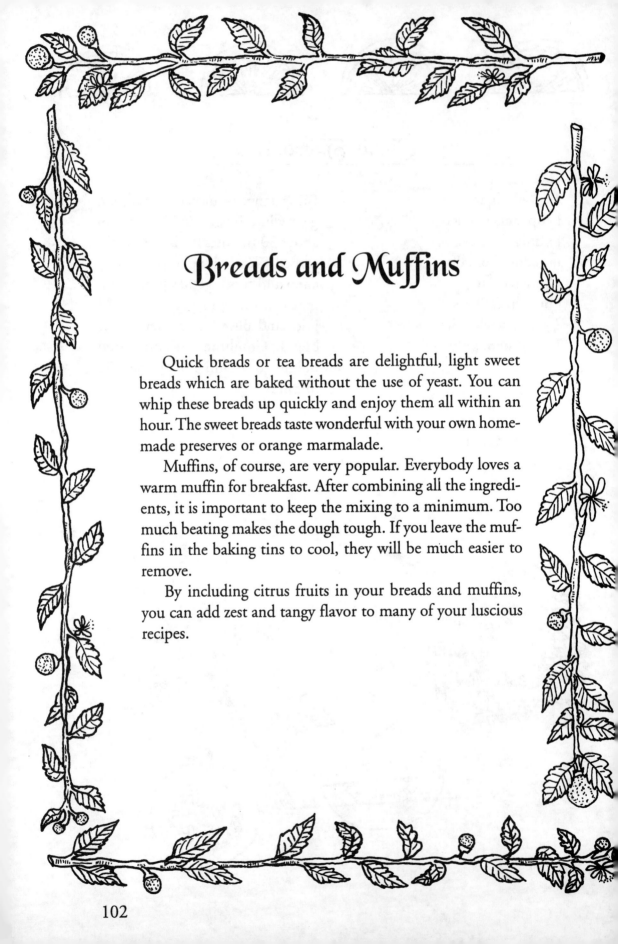

Breads and Muffins

Quick breads or tea breads are delightful, light sweet breads which are baked without the use of yeast. You can whip these breads up quickly and enjoy them all within an hour. The sweet breads taste wonderful with your own home-made preserves or orange marmalade.

Muffins, of course, are very popular. Everybody loves a warm muffin for breakfast. After combining all the ingredients, it is important to keep the mixing to a minimum. Too much beating makes the dough tough. If you leave the muffins in the baking tins to cool, they will be much easier to remove.

By including citrus fruits in your breads and muffins, you can add zest and tangy flavor to many of your luscious recipes.

Tropical Lemon Bread

¹/₄ cup butter

³/₄ cup sugar

2 eggs

3 teaspoons lemon rind

2 cups all-pupose flour

2¹/₂ teaspoons baking powder

1 teaspoon salt

³/₄ cup milk

¹/₂ cup walnut pieces

2 tablespoons lemon juice

2 tablespoons sugar

Cream together the butter and sugar. Add the eggs and lemon rind, beat well. Add dry ingredients to the wet mixture alternatively. Stir the walnuts in. Pour into a greased loaf pan and bake in a preheated oven at 350° for 1 hour. Combine the lemon juice and sugar and spread over the loaf while still warm.

Citrus Clue:

Add sliced fresh lemon to the top for a really zippy look.

Orange Nut Wreath

2 tablespoons sugar
1 teaspoon cinnamon
$^1/_4$ cup chopped dates
$^1/_4$ cup chopped walnuts
1 teaspoon grated orange peel
3 tablespoons fresh orange juice
2 drops vanilla
1 loaf frozen yeast bread,
   defrosted

Mix the sugar, dates, orange peel, juice, and nuts. Bring the mixture up to a boil, then reduce the heat and simmer for 5 minutes, stirring occasionally. Next, add the vanilla and roll out the dough to approximately 10" square. Spread the mixture onto the dough and roll the dough up and then bend it into a circle. Cut through the top in 1" slices. Sprinkle on a handful of nuts and sugar. Bake the wreath at 425° for 8 minutes.

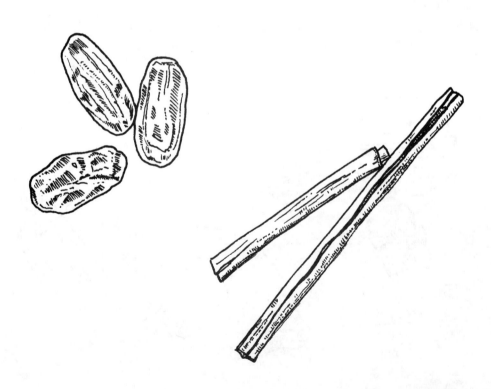

Fall Cranberry Orange Bread

2 cups diced cranberries
$\frac{1}{2}$ cup cooked pumpkin
$\frac{1}{4}$ cup margarine
$2\frac{1}{4}$ cups all-purpose flour
1 cup sugar
1 egg
$1\frac{1}{2}$ teaspoons baking powder
$\frac{1}{2}$ teaspoon baking soda
1 teaspoon salt
$\frac{1}{2}$ cup nuts
$\frac{3}{4}$ cup orange juice

Melt butter, remove from heat. Sift together flour, sugar, baking powder, and soda. Add juice, butter, and egg to flour mixture and stir until blended. Stir in pumpkin, nuts, and cranberries. Bake at 350° for 1 hour. Makes one loaf.

Macomber Fresh Apple, Orange Bread

1 cup apple, peeled and chopped
1 cup sugar
1/3 cup shortening, cream, or
    butter
1 egg
1/3 cup orange juice
2 cups all-purpose flour
1 teaspoon baking powder
1/2 teaspoon baking soda
3/4 cup raisins
1/4 cup nuts, chopped walnuts
    or pecans
1 teaspoon grated orange rind

Combine sugar, butter, and egg by using a spoon or rubber spatula. Add in order, while mixing between ingredients, juice, flour, baking powder, soda, raisins, walnuts, rind, and apple. Turn mixture into greased loaf pan. Bake 45 minutes in 350° oven. Yields one loaf.

Orange Drizzle Cranberry Bread

1 cup sugar
1/2 cup margarine
2 eggs
1/2 cup milk
2 cups all-purpose flour
2 teaspoons baking powder
3/4 cup fresh cranberries, chopped
1 1/2 teaspoons grated orange peel
1/2 cup chopped walnuts

Cream butter and sugar until light. Beat in eggs, one at a time, add milk. Combine flour and baking powder. Add to butter mixture, stir just until moist. Add cranberries, orange peel, and walnuts into batter. Grease 2 mini loaf pans. Put 1/2 cup batter into each pan. Bake at 375° for about 30 minutes. Cool on rack. Decorate or drizzle.

Orange Drizzle

1 1/2 tablespoons orange juice
1 cup confectioners sugar

Combine sugar and orange juice. Drizzle over each orange cranberry bread.

Orange Carrot Sweet Bread

$\frac{1}{2}$ cup butter
$1\frac{1}{2}$ cups sugar
4 egg whites (you don't need those yolks)
2 cups grated carrots
$\frac{1}{2}$ cup walnut pieces
1 teaspoon salt
1 teaspoon soda
1 tablespoon cinnamon
2 cups all-purpose flour

Cream together the butter, sugar, and egg whites. Stir in the carrots, orange juice, rind, and walnuts. Blend in the dry ingredients. Pour the batter into oiled loaf pans and bake at 350° for 40 minutes. To test: touch the middle of the cake and if done, the center will spring back. Makes two 9" loaves.

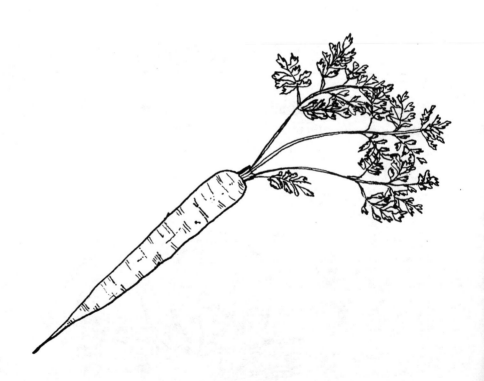

Zesty Lemon Muffins

4 cups all-purpose flour
3 teaspoons cinnamon
2 teaspoons baking soda
1/2 teaspoon ground cloves
2 cups sugar
1/2 cup butter
2 eggs
2 teaspoons lemon juice
2 cups apple sauce
2 tablespoons grated lemon rind
1 cup walnuts (chopped)

Mix the first 4 ingredients together. In a second bowl, cream together the sugar and butter until light and fluffy. Then add the eggs and lemon juice and beat. Stir the lemon rinds and walnuts into the applesauce. Gently stir the apple-lemon mixture into the butter mixture. Add this mixture to the dry ingredients and fold in. Spoon the mixture into a greased muffin pan and bake at 375° for 15 minutes. Cool the muffins on a wire rack. Makes 24 large or 36 small muffins.

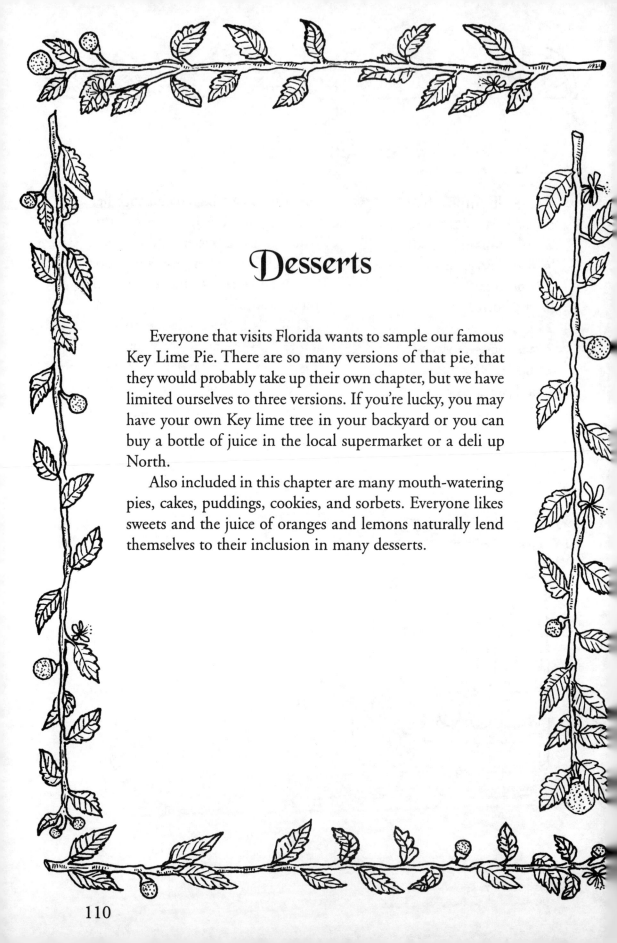

Desserts

Everyone that visits Florida wants to sample our famous Key Lime Pie. There are so many versions of that pie, that they would probably take up their own chapter, but we have limited ourselves to three versions. If you're lucky, you may have your own Key lime tree in your backyard or you can buy a bottle of juice in the local supermarket or a deli up North.

Also included in this chapter are many mouth-watering pies, cakes, puddings, cookies, and sorbets. Everyone likes sweets and the juice of oranges and lemons naturally lend themselves to their inclusion in many desserts.

Key Lime Pie Topped with Heaven

One 9 ounce graham cracker pie crust

6 ounces Key lime juice

2½ cups sweetened condensed milk

2 whole eggs

Heaven

2 cups whipping cream

2 tablespoons powdered sugar

1 teaspoon vanilla

Beat eggs and blend in milk. Add lime juice slowly while blending. Pour into pie shell and bake for 350° for 15 minutes or until light glaze appears on top. Let cool and refrigerate. Begin to whip cream. As cream thickens, add powdered sugar and vanilla. Beat until fluffy, then chill. Serve whipped heaven on top of pie slice. Decorate with a lime wedge or twist.

Citrus Clue:

Key limes are native to Malaya, India and the small round fruit is yellow inside and out. A true Key lime pie will be a lovely pale yellow.

Eula's Real Key Lime Pie

2¼ cups all-purpose flour
¾ tablespoon salt
¾ cup shortening (butter flavor)
5 tablespoons cold ice water

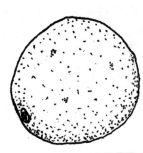 

Preheat the oven to 450°. Sift the flour and salt and using the hands, work in the shortening. Sprinkle in water and work in with your hands. Slowly add the water, until you form a ball. Separate the dough into two balls. Roll out one ball for each crust and place in a 9" pie pan. Freeze one unbaked crust in the pie pan. Use fingers to crimp the edges and prick the bottom and sides with fork. Bake at 450° and watch carefully until light brown. Makes 2 pie crusts.

ONE PIE FILLING

¾ cup sugar
4 heaping tablespoons cornstarch
¼ cup white corn syrup
3 large eggs, separate the whites for the meringue
¼ tablespoon salt
⅓ cup Key lime juice (no bottled juice, please) Eula says that it is fine to freeze fresh Key lime juice and use as needed.
⅔ cup hot water

Eula says, "You've got to work a little to have something good." Mix the sugar, salt, and starch. Then mix the egg yolks and syrup together with the sugar mixture. Combine together with ⅔ cup almost boiling water; add the lime juice slowly to this mixture until nicely blended. Set the mixture over a double boiler and after about 2 to 3 minutes, scrape the sides of the pot to see if thick. Carefully pour the filling into the baked pie crust. Let it set for 10 minutes.

MERINGUE

3 egg whites
6 tablespoons sugar

Beat the egg whites until beginning to stiffen and then add sugar until dissolved and very stiff. Put the meringue overlapping the edges of the pie, so it will not pull loose after baking. Fill in the top center with meringue. Bake at 350° until as dark as you like. Be sure to pour off "weeping," then the pie crust will stay crispy.

Citrus Clue:

Eula Rhodes is well-known on the Island for her Key lime pies.

Key Lime Cheesecake

2 eggs
6 tablespoons sugar
¼ cup Key lime juice (although regular lime juice will do)
¼ cup lemon juice
1 tablespoon gelatin (softened in 3 tablespoons cold water)
1½ cups cottage cheese
⅔ cup whipping cream
1 teaspoon butter
6 tablespoons finely crushed graham crackers

Beat the eggs and ¼ cup of the sugar. Stir in the juices. Stir over a double boiler until the mixture thickens and coats the spoon. Add the gelatin mixture and stir until dissolved. Cool and add the cottage cheese. Blend in the whipped cream. Whisk eggs and add remaining sugar. Fold the two mixtures together. Butter an 8" cake pan and sprinkle the bottom with the crushed graham crackers. Pour the mixture in and chill until firm. When ready to serve, turn over onto a serving plate.

Citrus Clue:
Serve with very thin slices of lemon or lime on the top.

Frozen Key Lime Tarts

$3/4$ cup oatmeal

$1/3$ cup brown sugar

$1/4$ cup melted butter

3 egg yolks, beaten

$1/4$ cup Key lime juice

$2/3$ cup sugar

$1/4$ teaspoon salt

2 teaspoons lime rind

$1 1/2$ teaspoon vanilla

3 egg whites, beaten to soft peaks

1 cup whopping cream, beaten until stiff

To make the crust, combine oatmeal, brown sugar, and melted butter. Spread on cookie sheet and toast for 350° for 10 minutes, stirring occasionally. Cool toss with fork while cooling. While the crust cools, prepare filling. Combine egg yolks, juice, sugar, and salt in saucepan. Cook over low heat, stirring constantly until it boils. Remove from heat, stir in rind and vanilla. Fold in egg whites, then cream. Put paper liners in muffin pans. Spoon 1 tablespoon crust in bottom, add 3 tablespoons filling, and top with 1 teaspoon crust. Place in freezer until ready to serve. Invert on plate and peel off paper.

Citrus Clue:

This recipe comes by way of Hale Herring and was always a treat when served visiting Granny Hale. As a great time saver—make a double batch, freeze, bag up, and store in the freezer.

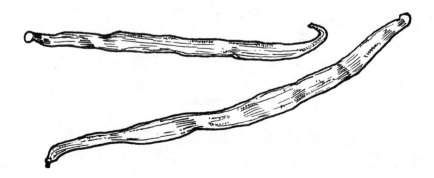

Mincemeat

6 cups raisins
$3^1/_2$ cups currants
$^1/_2$ cup dried apricots
$^1/_2$ cup dried peaches
$^3/_4$ cup dates
1 cup candied citrus peel
$^1/_2$ cup walnut pieces
$^1/_2$ cup almond pieces
1 pound Granny Smith apples
Juice of 3 lemons and grated rinds
$2^1/_4$ cups light brown sugar
1 cup butter (melted)
1 tablespoon allspice
$^1/_2$ cup Grand Marnier

In a large bowl, place the raisins and currants. Chop up the apricots, peaches, dates, peel, nuts, and apples. Mix together all ingredients and the lemon juice and grated rind. Stir in the brown sugar, butter, spice, and Grand Marnier. Stir the mixture until evenly blended. Cover with plastic wrap and refrigerate for two days. Use 6 (1 pint) sterilized jars and lids. Spoon in the mincemeat mixture and fill to the top. Cover with sealing paraffin and seal.

Citrus Clue:

Mincemeat is traditional English Christmas food. It is usually made into mince pies, which are topped with hard sauce or whipped cream. Mincemeat has been around for centuries and was used in Medieval times, particularly during Lent. Meat was not allowed to be eaten then, so dried fruits were a staple part of the diet.

Orange Hard Sauce

1½ cups powdered sugar
2-5 tablespoons butter (stop when it is the consistency that you like)
1-2 tablespoons orange juice (Again, this depends on how much orange flavor you like)
¼ cup cream (optional)

Blend the butter until soft and slowly add the sifted powdered sugar. You may adjust the butter to suit your taste. Then slowly add the juice, until the sauce is very smooth. Chill thoroughly in the refrigerator.

Citrus Clue:

Great with mince pies or Christmas pudding. Part of a hardy English tradition.

Sanibel Lemon Mist Pie

3 eggs (separated)
$^2/_3$ cup sugar ($^1/_3$ cup in 2 containers)
Pinch of salt
3 teaspoons grated lemon rind
7 tablespoons lemon juice
3 tablespoons boiling water
3 tablespoons lemon gelatin
$^1/_2$ teaspoon cream of tartar
One 8" pie shell

Beat the egg yolks slightly. Stir in $^1/_3$ cup sugar. Add salt, lemon juice, and rind. Cook this mixture over a double boiler; make sure to stir constantly until the mixture thickens. If you don't keep stirring, you know you'll have a gooey mess to clean up. Put the gelatin in a small bowl and add boiling water. Mix together the gelatin with the custard. Cool until the mixture stars to gel. Beat slightly and set aside while making meringue. Beat the egg whites until they are stiff and then slowly add the remaining sugar. Continue beating the mixture until it is stiff and glossy. Fold the meringue into the custard. Place mixture in the pie shell and chill in the refrigerator overnight.

Sunset Lemon Apple Pie

$1^1/_2$ pounds of Granny Smith's apples

Grated rind of one lemon

$^1/_4$ teaspoon clove

$^1/_4$ teaspoon cinnamon

3 tablespoons sugar

One 8" pie shell (top and bottom required)

1 tablespoon sugar

1 teaspoon allspice

Peel, core, and slice the apples. Place them in a sauce pan with the grated rind, spices, 3 tablespoons of sugar, and 1 tablespoon of water. Cover and cook until the apples are mushy. Remove from the heat and cool. Remove the rind. Put the cooled filling into the base of the pie shell. Brush the edges of the pie shell with milk and cover with pastry lid. Seal the edges firmly with the back of a fork. Brush the pastry top with milk. Mix 1 tablespoon sugar with 1 teaspoon allspice and sprinkle on the top. Place the pie on a cookie sheet and bake in an oven at 350° for 35-40 minutes or until the pastry is golden brown.

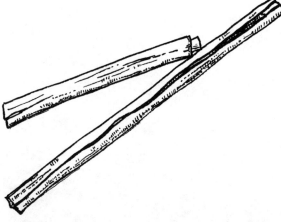

Lime Sponge Cake Pie

1 cup sugar
1 tablespoon all-purpose flour
Pinch salt
2 tablespoons butter
2 eggs
1 cup milk
1 lime
1 teaspoon lime rind

Cream sugar, butter, flour, and salt. Add egg yolks, juice of lime, and grated rind. Beat egg whites until almost stiff. Fold in batter and bake in pie pan at 350° for 30-45 minutes.

The Sunshine Cafe Blackberry, Strawberry, and Lime Cobbler

2 pints strawberries, washed, capped, and halved
2 pints blackberries, washed
Juice of 2 limes
³/₄ cup granulated sugar

In a large bowl, combine above ingredients and transfer to a 13" x 9" x 2" cake pan.

COBBLER TOPPING

3 tablespoon unsalted butter
³/₄ cup granulated sugar
1¹/₂ cups cake flour
2 teaspoons baking soda
1 teaspoon cream of tartar
1 teaspoon salt
¹/₂ cup buttermilk
1 large egg

Preheat oven to 350°. In a mixer with paddle attachment, whip butter and sugar at high speed for 5 minutes. Add the egg and whip for 3 minutes. Add baking soda, cream of tartar, salt, and half of flour. Mix for 30 seconds, add half of buttermilk and mix another 30 seconds. Scrap bowl and add remaining flour and buttermilk, mix at high speed for 5 minutes. With a large rubber spatula, drop the batter on the fruit with a slow sweeping motion. Be sure to leave a 1" strip around the edge as the batter will expand. Bake for 40-45 minutes or until golden brown.

Citrus Clue:

At The Sunshine Café on Captiva Island, we served this cobbler warm with vanilla ice cream, but it's also great with warm heavy cream.

Orange Frosting

5 tablespoons butter
Juice of one orange
3$\frac{1}{2}$ cups of powdered sugar
$\frac{1}{2}$ teaspoon vanilla

Blend the butter, orange juice, vanilla, and powdered sugar until very smooth. Spread on you luscious cake!

Lemony Cream Cheese Icing

$\frac{1}{2}$ cup butter
8 oz. cream cheese (It's OK to use light cream cheese.)
3 tablespoons lemon juice
4 cups powdered sugar

Cream together the butter and cream cheese. Beat in the rest of the ingredients until smooth.

 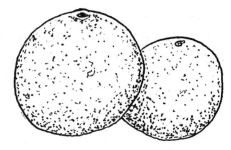

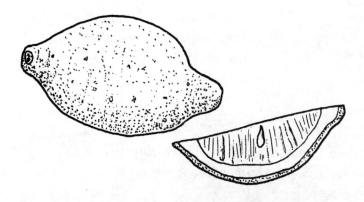

122

Lemony Cake

1 package lemon cake mix
1 package lemon pudding mix
4 eggs
1 cup lemon-lime soda
$^2/_3$ cup oil
1 cup walnuts
Juice of lemon and grated peel

Combine all the ingredients and mix according to cake mix directions. Pour mixture into bundt cake pan. Bake for 45-60 minutes according to the cake mix directions. Cool and ice with lemon icing.

LEMON ICING

2 cups powdered sugar
$^1/_2$ cup lemon juice
$^1/_2$ cup margarine

Combine all the ingredients and blend until smooth. Spread on the cooled lemon cake.

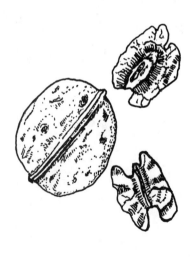

Orange Almond Cake

1 cup fresh soft bread crumbs
Grated rind of orange
Juice of 3 oranges
1 cup ground almonds
4 eggs
$\frac{1}{2}$ cup sugar
Confectioners sugar
Whipped cream (optional)

Mix together the bread crumbs, rind, juice, and ground almonds. Beat the egg yolks and sugar until creamy and add to mixture. Beat the egg whites until stiff and fold gently into the cake mixture. Grease a 7" cake pan and add mixture. Bake at 325° for approximately 50 minutes. Allow it to cool and put in a cool place until firm. Dust with confectioner's sugar, or top with whipped cream.

Florida Snowball Cake

1 angel food cake
2 envelopes gelatin
4 tablespoons cold water
1 cup boiling water
1 cup orange sections
1 cup orange juice
1 cup sugar
$\frac{1}{2}$ teaspoon salt
2 tablespoons lemon juice
3 packages powdered whipped topping

Dissolve the gelatin in cold water. Add the boiling water until the gelatin is completely dissolved. Add the orange juice, sugar, lemon juice, and salt. Refrigerate until the gelatin starts to gel. Beat 2 packages of powdered whip topping and fold into mixture. Fold in the orange sections. Take the angel food cake and break into pieces. Place them in alternate layers with the gelatin mixture. Top with a final layer of whipped topping after refrigerating for a day.

Orange Marmalade Shortbread

$1/3$ cup sugar
$2/3$ cup butter
1 cup all-purpose flour
3 tablespoons orange marmalade

Preheat the oven to 300°. Blend together the sugar and the butter until nice and smooth. Add flour and mix until paste-like. Finally, add the marmalade and completely mix in. Spread the paste into a small round or square baking pan. Prong the edges with a fork and dust with sugar. Put in the oven and bake slowly—usually 30 to 45 minutes, but make sure that the shortbread is a beautiful golden brown. Remove from the oven and cool for 10 minutes before cutting into squares. Leave to cool in the pan.

Citrus Clue:

If you put the shortbread in an airtight container, it will remain crisp for quite awhile.

Yogurt Orange Cookies

1½ cups sugar
1 cup butter
3 eggs
1 teaspoon salt
1 cup yogurt
1 teaspoon baking soda
1 teaspoon baking powder
3¾ cups all-purpose flour
Juice and grated rind of an orange

Cream the sugar and the butter. Add eggs and whip it until light. Add salt, yogurt, orange juice, and rind. Add 1 cup of flour and stir. Add baking soda and powder with the next cup of flour and gradually stir in all the flour. Drop by the teaspoon on to an oiled cookie sheet. Bake at 350° for approximately 10 minutes. They will spring back from a light touch. When cooled, you can frost them with an orange frosting.

Jeweled Rocks

2 cups all-purpose flour
$\frac{1}{2}$ teaspoon salt
2 teaspoons baking powder
4 tablespoons butter
$\frac{1}{4}$ cup sugar
$\frac{1}{2}$ cup candied citrus peel
$\frac{1}{2}$ teaspoon orange zest
1 egg
2 tablespoons orange juice

Preheat the oven to 400°. Grease the baking sheet. Sift the flour, salt, and baking powder together. Rub in the butter so that the mixture resembles bread crumbs. Add the citrus peel and orange zest. Next, beat the egg and add it to the flour mixture. Add the orange juice and mix well. Make 12 rough uneven mounds on the baking sheet. Bake for 20 minutes. Cool on a wire rack. Makes 12.

Citrus Clue:

This recipe is a tasty British drop biscuit and is served like scones.

Dover Marmalade Cookies

1 cup orange marmalade
2 eggs
¹/₂ cup melted butter
¹/₂ cup sugar
2 cups all-purpose flour
1 teaspoon baking soda
¹/₂ cup chopped pecans and
   currants

Mix marmalade and eggs. Mix butter, sugar, flour, soda, pecans, and currants. Combine two mixtures. Drop from spoon on greased baking sheet. Bake in 400° oven about 5 minutes. Watch till golden brown.

Citrus Clue:

These cookies store well. The recipe originated from Dover-Foxcraft, a small town in Maine.

Lemon Pecan Cookies

³/₄ cup butter
1 cup sugar
1 egg
2 teaspoons lemon peel (grated)
1 cup pecans
2 tablespoons lemon juice
2 cups all-purpose flour
1 teaspoon baking powder
¹/₂ teaspoon salt

Cream together the butter and sugar, then add the egg, lemon juice, and peel. Sift the flour, baking powder, and salt together and add to the creamed mixture. Stir in the nuts and roll the mixture into two logs. Chill thoroughly. Slice the dough into thin slices and bake at 350° for 10 to 12 minutes.

Citrus Clue:

Lemons were transported to Europe from their homeland of India by early Arabic traders.

Tropical Lemon Squares

$^2/_3$ cup butter

$1^1/_2$ cups all-purpose flour

4 eggs

2 cups brown sugar

$1^1/_2$ cups coconut

$^1/_4$ teaspoon baking powder

1 teaspoon vanilla

$1^1/_3$ cups powdered sugar

2 tablespoons lemon rind

3 tablespoons lemon juice

Mix the butter and the flour together. Pat into a 13" x 9" baking pan. Bake at 350° for 20 minutes. In the meantime, beat the eggs, sugar, coconut, baking powder, and vanilla together. Pat the mixture onto the baked crust and return to oven. Bake for an additional 25-30 minutes. Blend the powdered sugar and the lemon juice and frost the squares, while still warm.

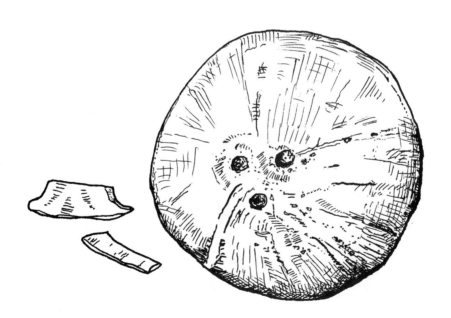

L'Orange Cheesecake Brownies

FILLING

One package, 8 ounces cream
  cheese, softened
¼ cup orange marmalade
2 tablespoons sugar
1 egg

BROWNIES

¾ cup shortening
4 squares cooking chocolate,
  melted
2 cups sugar
4 eggs
1½ cups all-purpose flour
1 teaspoon baking powder
1 teaspoon vanilla
1 cup chopped walnuts

Preheat oven to 350°. Grease 9" x 12" baking pan. Beat cream cheese, marmalade, sugar, and egg with mixer until smooth. Set aside filling. Mix shortening, chocolate, sugar, eggs, vanilla, and beat thoroughly. Add flour, baking powder, and beat some more. Pour ⅔ of brownie batter into pan. Drop spoonfuls of filling onto batter. Pour rest of batter into pan. Use a knife to thinly cut through batter. This creates a beautiful swirl effect. Bake 30 minutes.

Citrus Clue:

If in a rush, use a large package of brownie mix.

Bootles Pudding

¹/₄ cup sherry
Pound cake
2 oranges, juice and rinds, grated
1 lemon, juice and grated rind
1 - 2 tablespoons sugar
1 cup whipping cream
Toasted almonds or coconut,
  optional

Put the sugar into a mixing bowl and add the juice and grated rinds. Whip the cream and fold in the juices. Cut up the pound cake and put into a pretty glass bowl. Sprinkle with the sherry. Pour in the cream and juice mixture. Put into the refrigerator overnight. Serve the next day, but beforehand, you may like to garnish with toasted almonds or coconut.

Citrus Clue:
Kate's mom, Libby Hayes, gave her this luscious English recipe.

Sanibel Dream Pudding

2 tablespoons butter or margarine
$\frac{1}{4}$ cup sugar
3 tablespoons all-purpose flour
Juice and rind of 3 Key limes (or 1 lemon)
2 eggs
1 cup milk

Cream together the butter and sugar and add the flour. Add the juice, rind, and slightly beaten egg yolks. Stir in the milk and fold in stiffly beaten egg whites. Place in a buttered oven-proof dish and put in a roasting pan of hot water. Bake in the oven at 350° for 30 minutes.

Orange Meringue Dessert

5 egg whites
1¼ cups sugar
1 cup home-made orange
    marmalade
1 cup whipping cream
½ cup sour cream

Grease a shallow baking tray 10" x 15" then cover with wax paper. In a bowl, whisk the egg whites until stiff. Beat in ½ the sugar, then gently stir in the remaining sugar. Spread the egg mixture on the wax paper. Bake in oven for 10 minutes at 400°. Whisk the whipping cream until thick. Add the marmalade and the sour cream to the cream. Remove the meringue from the oven and allow to cool for 2 minutes then turn onto wax paper that has been dredged with sugar. Peel off the cooked wax paper, and allow to cool completely. Spread the marmalade cream on the meringue. Using the sugared wax paper under the meringue, roll up the meringue. Serves 8.

Tangelo Mousse

1 packet of unflavored gelatin
2 cups of freshly squeezed tangerine juice
Skinned segments from 2 tangerines
One 8 ounce can of evaporated milk, well chilled

Make up gelatin using tangerine juice instead of water. Leave to cool but not set. Beat evaporated milk until white and fluffy. Beat in cooled tangerine gelatin. Gently stir in tangerine segments. Place in individual glass bowls. Serves 6-8.

Citrus Clue:

Orange juice may be substitute for the tangerine juice.

Orange Dream Dessert

2 teaspoons gelatin
1¼ cups freshly squeezed orange juice
2 egg yolks
6 tablespoons sugar
1¼ cups whipping cream
4 tablespoons Cointreau
1 orange

Dissolve the gelatin in 2 tablespoons of orange juice that has been boiled. Add the remaining orange juice and stir until the gelatin is well mixed. Whisk the egg yolks with the sugar, until it is thick and creamy. Combine the gelatin and the egg mixture. Pour into individual dishes. Grate the rind from the orange. Cut the orange into thin slices, being careful to remove the "pith." Place the sliced oranges on the top of the cream dessert and sprinkle on the grated orange rind. Cool in the refrigerator before serving. Serves 4.

Citrus Clue:

Jean, who hails from England, says the "pith" is the English term for the white inner layer of the rind.

 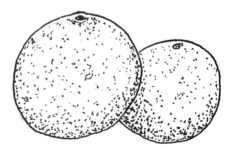

Orange and Strawberry Gel

1¼ cups water
1¼ cups fresh orange juice
2 teaspoons grated orange rind
¾ cup sugar
1 envelope gelatin (dissolved in 2 tablespoons water)
1 pint fresh strawberries (cleaned and stemmed)

Divide the strawberries between six tall wine glasses. Bring the water, juice, rind, and sugar to a boil. Stir in the gelatin. Leave it to cool, then strain. Pour into the glasses. Serves 6.

Sugarless, Orange-Tangerine Gelatin

1 cup chilled tangerine juice
4 ounces gelatin; plain
3 cups orange juice

In bowl, add gelatin to chilled juice, set aside. Heat 3 cups orange juice. Add hot juice to gelatin mixture and stir well. Chill in 13" x 9" cake pan. This dessert has no refined sugar or artificial colorings. Other juices can be substituted.

Citrus Clue:

For extra elegance, you may add a sprig of mint to the top of each dessert and orange zest to decorate. It is excellent partially frozen, too!

Zesty Meringue

4 egg whites
1 cup of sugar
$\frac{1}{2}$ cup of puffed rice
Zest of 1 orange
$\frac{1}{2}$ pint heavy whipping cream
2 tablespoons sugar
3 tablespoons brandy
4 tangerines, peeled and segmented

Preheat oven to 250°, then grease and line 2 baking trays with waxed paper marked with an 8" circle, a 7" circle, and a 5" circle. Beat egg whites until stiff, adding $\frac{1}{2}$ cup of the sugar, a tablespoon at a time, beating well between spoonfuls. Fold in remaining sugar (reserve 1 tablespoon) with puffed rice and zest. Spread the meringue over the 3 circles, sprinkling the smallest circle with the reserved sugar. Bake on low shelf in the oven for 3 and a half to 4 hours until crisp. Remove from oven and peel away waxed paper and place meringues on wire rack. Whip cream and sugar together, stir in brandy. Spread cream on the 2 larger meringues and top with tangerine sections. Layer the meringues, from big to small and decorate with tangerine segments.

Citrus Clue:
Meringue circles may be stored in airtight containers until ready to spread with the cream.

Orange Sorbet

1 quart hot water
1 quart sugar
³/₄ cup orange juice
¹/₂ cup lemon juice

Combine sugar and hot water. Stir until sugar is dissolved. Take 2 cups of cooled simple syrup (sugar water mixture) and add orange juice and lemon juice. Mix well and place in freezer overnight.

Lemon, Banana, and Orange Sorbet

2 cups sugar
3 cups water
3 bananas, mashed
3 oranges
3 lemons

Mix together the sugar and water until the sugar is dissolved. Wash the oranges and lemons, peel and section them into small pieces. Mash the bananas and add the fruit to the sugar water. Place in an air-tight container in the freezer and enjoy when frozen.

Hot Chocolate-Orange Fudge Sauce

Two 1 ounce chocolate squares
1½ cups sugar
½ cup milk
Zest of 1 orange
2 tablespoons butter or margarine
½ teaspoon vanilla

Over a low heat, combine the chocolate squares, sugar, and milk. Heat gently until the chocolate is melted. Add the zest of the orange and the butter. Continue to boil gently for approximately 8 minutes. DO NOT STIR WHILE BOILING! Finally, add the vanilla when the sauce is cooler. This mixture becomes quite thick when cooled, but you can warm it up just before serving.

Citrus Clue:

This chocolate sauce is lovely served over French Vanilla ice cream or frozen yogurt. The sauce can be kept for quite a while in the refrigerator, but it probably will not stay around too long!

Tangerine in Syrup

3 cups tangerine sections, remove membrane

3 cups sugar

1 cup water

Place the tangerine sections into serving dishes. In a large pot, dissolve sugar and water. Boil for 15 minutes or until the syrup is formed. Pour syrup over tangerine sections.

Citrus Clue:

Tangerine in Syrup is wonderful over ice cream. This has been approved by all my children. Tastes great with orange or grapefruit. Gramp enjoys it instead of sugar in his ice tea.

Gardening Tips, Decorating, and Craft Ideas

One of the most wonderful attributes of living in Florida is the abundance of citrus. There is no finer way to start the day than with a glass of freshly squeezed orange juice, especially if it comes from your own backyard. However, boredom quickly settles in when your tree has produced enough fruit for you and all of your relatives to have several glasses of orange juice for the rest of their natural lives.

This section is about utilizing a bountiful harvest whether from your own backyard, your neighbors yard, or the local fruit stand. It provides hints for the home gardener and craft ideas.

One of the first satisfactions of being a Florida home owner is adding a citrus tree to your yard. Depending on the size of the yard, your landscaping, and location, the home gardener has a wonderful selection of citrus to choose from. If you were lucky, there was already a citrus tree on your property. An ideal yard will have an orange, tangerine, tangelo, grapefruit, lemon, and lime.

Planting Guide for Citrus Trees

Dig a hole two times the width of the pot and one-and-a-half pots deep. Amend the soil removed from the hole with organic materials such as compost or cow manure approximately 25% compost to 75% soil. Place pot in prepared hole and plant so tree is even with top of mound. Water and tap soil in firmly. Do not fertilize trees when planting! Keep the soil clear of weeds or grass for area of the tree's canopy. Water everyday for the first week after planting and then about once a week depending on the amount of rain.

Citrus Trees

Oranges	Ripen
Blood	December-March
Hamlin	October-January
King	February-March
Navel	September-December
Page	October-December
Pineapple	December-February
Parson Brown	October-December
Queen	December-March
Valencia	March-July

Tangelos	Ripen
Nova	October-December
Orlando	October-December
Minneola	January-March
Honey Bell	January-March

Tangerines	Ripen
Dancy	December-February
Lee	November-December
Oneco	January-March
Ponkan	October-January
Robinson	September-October
Satsuma	October-December
Murcott	February-April
Sun Burst	November-December

Grapefruits	Ripen
Duncan	October-January
Marsh White	December-April
Pink Marsh	October-February
Ruby Red	October-January
Redblush	October-March
Thomson Pink	October-January

Lemons	Ripen
Bearss	December-April
Meyer	December-April
Ponderosa	November-March

Limes	Ripen
Key Lime	November-April
Persian	April-September

Miscellaneous	Ripen
Calamondin	October-January
Citrons	Fall-Spring
Kumquats	October-February

Freeze warnings: Leave unripened fruit on the tree. The flavor of citrus will not improve once it is removed from the tree. Fruit that freezes and doesn't fall from the tree is still edible and good for juice.

Holiday Decorating with Citrus

For an easy festive look for the holidays, fill bowls with fresh citrus to add color to any decor. You can use bowls with a mixture of texture and color. Tuck gold, silver, or red bows amongst the fruit or tie a bright bow around your basket or bowl of fruit.

Pomanders

1 box whole cloves
1 dozen Ponderosa lemons
Bamboo skewers

Ponderosas make excellent pomanders because of their thick skin. Use skewers to prick patterns in the lemon and fill holes with studs. Try not to punch the hole too far into the pulp or the fruit will seep and you will soon have a moldy mess.

Citrus Clue:

This makes a great holiday project for the kids and makes wonderful hostess gifts! Simply wrap pomander in clear plastic wrap and tie both ends with bows.

Citrus Vases

Assortment of oranges, lemons, and grapefruits
Florist water tubes
Grapefruit corer

Select large fruit and carefully trim a small amount of rind off the bottom, being careful to not cut the pith, so that fruit rests evenly and won't roll. Use grapefruit corer to make an opening three-quarters of the way through the center of fruit. Remove rubber top from tubes and place florist water tube into the opening. Chose flowers on fairly short stems or light in weight so the vase is not top heavy. Fill tubes $^2/_3$ full with water or florist solution. Replace rubber top and push selected flowers or greenery into tubes.

Citrus Clue:

This is a great way to show off your prize hibiscus or keep sprigs of kitchen herbs handy. These throw away vases are a great way to add color and fragrance to any decor.

Citus Grapevine Wreath

1 large grapevine wreath
1 Ponderosa lemon
2 temple oranges
3 limes
2 Key limes
6 calamondins or kumquats
Lemon leaves
Hot glue gun

If you make your own wreath, leave some leaves on the vines as you wrap the wreath for greenery. Wash fruit and rub till they shine, like polishing an apple. Decide top and bottom of wreath. Apply hot glue in center of southwest corner and push ponderosa lemon into glue firmly. Arrange oranges around base of lemon and secure to wreath with glue. Place limes around base of oranges and secure with glue. Apply glue in empty spaces and fill with key limes, lemon leaves, citrons or kumquats. Trim with a bright holiday bow.

Citrus Clue:

Add a few shells and you will truly have a Barrier Island holiday wreath. You can also use a smaller wreath and make table arrangements!

Orange Simmering Potpourri

$\frac{1}{2}$ cup dried orange peel
$\frac{1}{4}$ cup dried cranberries
4 cinnamon sticks
1 tablespoon cloves
1 nutmeg, broken into pieces
1 tablespoon whole spice

Mix ingredients together. Put half the mixture in 2 cups water and simmer in a saucepan or in a simmering potpourri pot. Just cover the mixture with water and light the pot.

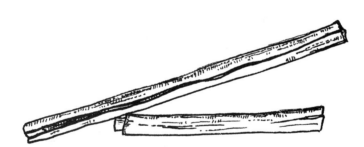

Dried Orange Slice Wreath

5 oranges
2 feet of string
5 sticks of cinnamon

Cut the oranges into quarter-inch slices. Dry in the oven for 3 to 8 hours at 250° or in a food dryer. When all the slices are evenly dried, thread the string through their centers leaving at least 4" at one end. Tie the ends together and form a circle. Cut off the excess string. With very thin string or even dental floss, tie on the cinnamon sticks at regular intervals.

Citrus Clue:

For Christmas tree trimming, tie individual orange slices with ribbon, or string with cranberries and popcorn for a garland. To make your own potpourri, combine dried orange slices with lime and lemon slices and bits of cinnamon sticks.

Orange Candles

1 orange
2" candle wick
Vegetable oil (not olive)
Thumb tack

Cut the orange in half so the end of each half sits flat. Scoop out the pulp. You could utilize the pulp in another recipe. Carefully tack a wick into the bottom of the orange rind cup. Pour in the oil (approximately $\frac{1}{4}$ cup). Cut a 1" diameter hole in the top half. Place the top half of the orange on the bottom. Light the wick and enjoy the fragrance.

Citrus Clue:

The orange rind cups make great 9"candle holders. Make the top half opening slightly smaller than the candle diameter. Put the two halves together, push the candle through the top opening and viola! Adds refreshing beauty to your table.

Citrus Potpourri

1 cup orange peel shapes, dried
$\frac{1}{2}$ cup lemon peel shapes, dried
$\frac{1}{2}$ cup almonds in shells
6 cinnamon sticks, halved
1 cup wood chips
Few drops of orange oil
$\frac{1}{2}$ cup of orange colored dried flowers

Dry peels on a cookie sheet at 200° for 5-10 hours (leave oven cracked open). Place ingredients, except cinnamon sticks, in a large jar. Screw on lid tightly and shake. Place in a cool dark place for 2 weeks, shaking jar daily. Place desired amount of potpourri and cinnamon sticks in container, basket, or shallow dish. Replace lid on jar and keep remaining potpourri in the dark until required.

Decorative Christmas Gift Wrap

Dried lime slices
Pasta bows
White freezer paper
Hot glue gun
Red latex paint

Wrap packages in white paper, shiny side inside. Arrange lime circles to form Christmas tree by centering one lime circle, then place two circles underneath, followed by three circles and glue in place. Paint bows red with latex paint and when dry place one in each circle. Stack two or three at base of tree to form a trunk.

Citrus Clue
You can also use dried citrus leaves to fill in or shape a wreath.

Natural Fine China Cleaner

$\frac{1}{2}$ teaspoon salt
$\frac{1}{2}$ teaspoon lemon juice

Put salt and lemon juice in cup. Use fingers to create a paste. Use paste to clean coffee stains in china cups.

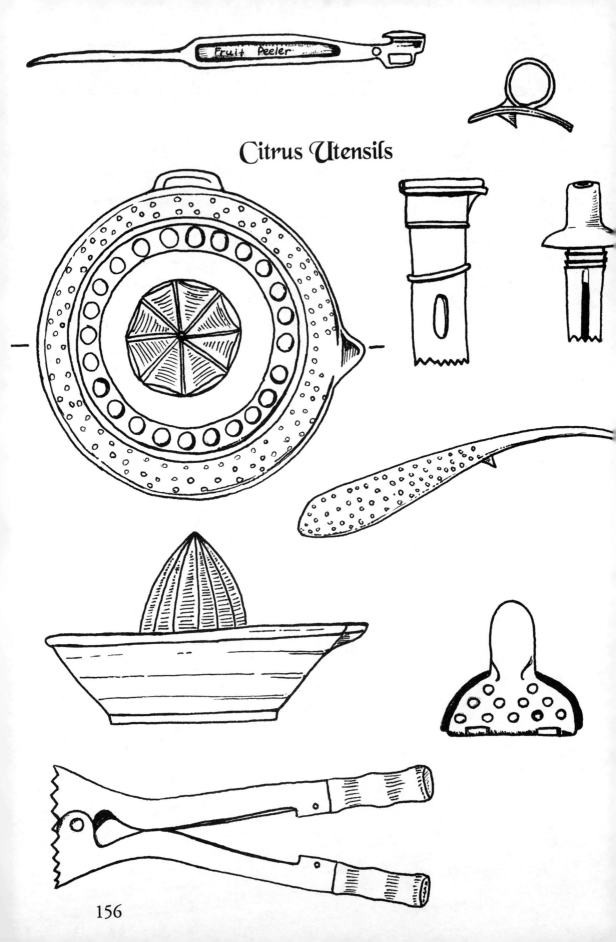

Citrus Utensils

American/European Conversion Chart

Volume

¼ cup	=	2 fl. oz./60 ml.
⅓ cup	=	3 fl. oz./85 ml.
½ cup	=	4 fl. oz./125 ml.
⅔ cup	=	6 fl. oz./170 ml.
1 cup	=	8 fl. oz./250 ml.
2 cups	=	16 fl. oz./500 ml.

Spoonful Equivalents

⅛ teaspoon	=	.5 ml.
¼ teaspoon	=	1.5 ml.
½ teaspoon	=	3 ml.
1 teaspoon	=	5 ml.
1 tablespoon	=	15 ml.

Oven Temperature

Fahrenheit		Centigrade
250F	=	130C
300F	=	150C
325F	=	165C
350F	=	175C
375F	=	190C
400F	=	205C

Weight

1 ounce	=	28 grams
8 ounces	=	225 grams
12 ounces	=	340 grams
1 pound	=	450 grams

Recipe List